SOCIAL PROCESSES

Bureaucracy
Dennis Warwick
University of Leeds

Social Control
C. Ken Watkins
University of Leeds

Communication
Prof. Denis McQuail
University of Amsterdam

Stratification
Prof. R. K. Kelsall
University of Sheffield
and *H. Kelsall*

Industrialism
Barry Turner
University of Exeter

Social Change
Anthony Smith
University of Reading

Socialisation
Graham White
University of Liverpool

Social Conflict
Prof. John Rex
University of Aston

Forthcoming titles will include:

Migration
Prof. J. A. Jackson
University of Dublin

SOCIAL RESEARCH

The Limitations of Social Research
Prof. M. D. Shipman
University of Warwick

Social Research Design
Prof. E. Krausz
University of Newcastle
and
S. H. Miller
City University

Sources of Official Data
Kathleen Pickett
University of Liverpool

History of Social Research Methods
Gary Easthope
University of East Anglia

Deciphering Data
Jonathan Silvey
University of Nottingham

The Philosophy of Social Research
John Hughes
University of Lancaster

Data Collection in Context
Stephen Ackroyd
and
John Hughes
University of Lancaster

Leisure

KENNETH ROBERTS B.SC. (SOC.), M.SC. (ECON.)
Senior Lecturer in Sociology
University of Liverpool

Second edition

Longman London and New York

Longman Group Limited
Longman House
Burnt Mill, Harlow, Essex UK

Published in the United States of America
by Longman Inc., New York

© Longman Group Limited 1970, 1981

First published 1970
Second edition 1981

British Library Cataloguing in Publication Data

Roberts, Kenneth, 1940-
    Leisure. – 2nd ed. – (Aspects of modern sociology:
    the social structure of modern Britain).
    1. Leisure – Social aspects
    I. Title   II. Series
    306'.4   GV181.3   80-42055

    ISBN 0-582-29556-4

Printed in Great Britain by
Butler & Tanner Ltd, Frome and London

CONTENTS

EDITORS' PREFACE

This series has been designed to meet the needs of students following a variety of academic and professional courses in universities, polytechnics, colleges of higher education, colleges of education, and colleges of further education. Although principally of interest to social scientists, the series does not attempt a comprehensive treatment of the whole field of sociology, but concentrates on the social structure of modern Britain which forms a central feature of most such tertiary level courses in this country. Its purpose is to offer an analysis of our contemporary society through the study of basic demographic, ideological and structural features, and the examination of such major social institutions as the family, education, the economic and political structure and religion. The aim has been to produce a series of introductory texts which will in combination form the basis for a sustained course of study, but each volume has been designed as a single whole and can be read in its own right.

We hope that the topics covered in the series will prove attractive to a wide reading public and that, in addition to students, others who wish to know more than is readily available about the nature and structure of their own society will find them of interest.

John Barron Mays
Maurice Craft

FOREWORD

This is a completely rewritten version of the book that first appeared in 1970. The changes take account of subsequent developments in society at large, and in the academic study of leisure. Since 1970 there has been a major growth of leisure research. Most of the studies quoted in this volume have appeared only during the last 10 years. But this book is a revised edition rather than a totally new piece of work since the main arguments of the original volume are developed and enlarged, not contradicted or replaced. In my unrepentant view, recent trends and research confirm the key propositions of the earlier edition; that leisure is growing, that its uses are being released from determination by occupational and other statuses, and that leisure is becoming less of a residual part and more of a pervasive quality of life. The following pages do not retract but refine and consolidate these arguments.

I should like to record my appreciation to the Editors of the Series for their consistent support, and to the numerous leisure scholars, in Britain and abroad, with whom I have been privileged to work, whose arguments have stimulated the development of my own ideas and made the sociology of leisure such an exciting area. Last, but by no means least, my thanks are due to Patricia McMillan and Bey Bath who typed the manuscript. Needless to say, the author accepts sole responsibility for any errors and omissions in the evidence and arguments to follow.

Kenneth Roberts

BY THE SAME AUTHOR

From School to Work (*1971*)
Strike at Pilkingtons (*joint author, 1971*)
The Character-Training Industry (*joint author, 1974*)
The Fragmentary Class Structure (*joint author, 1977*)
The Working Class (*1978*)
Contemporary Society and the Growth of Leisure (*1978*)
Sociology and Leisure Research (*1980*)

1

LEISURE AND SOCIOLOGY

Why study leisure or anything else? The intellectual challenge can contain its own justification. The study of leisure, like sports and games themselves, can be practised for its own sake, but it has usually been inspired by an overriding social purpose – a commitment to address the 'problem of leisure', however defined. In Britain leisure research has developed mainly within the Fabian, social betterment tradition, predicated on the assumption that once the facts about poverty, disease and crime, plus uses and abuses of leisure time, become known, action and improvement may follow.

It has always been foolish to dimiss leisure as trivial, unworthy of serious discussion. American researchers have diagnosed their public's perceptions of life's quality. They have even attempted to measure 'happiness' by sampling people's feelings about life in general and many of its specific aspects including their health, marriages, education and jobs. One clear conclusion to emerge is that the areas that contribute most powerfully to the individual's overall sense of well-being are close and personal. The national economy, politics and international relations, the kind of issues that have hitherto preoccupied serious-minded social scientists, neither disturb nor elate the proverbial man in the street. His sense of well-being depends more on the state of his marriage and his opportunities to experience fun and enjoyment.[1] Neither the American nor British publics place leisure at the top of the list when asked to name the things most important in their quality of life. Houses, jobs, income and education receive more 'votes'. But satisfaction with leisure correlates more strongly with general life satisfaction than any other single component.[2]

In Britain the Sports Council has vigorously defended itself against those who attempt to dismiss leisure as frivolous. 'It was put to us that worrying about recreation and sports provision is to worry about palliatives and to avoid the really crucial issues of homes and jobs. Good homes and satisfying jobs are vital: but there is plenty of anecdotal and research evidence that as soon as these are provided, human beings expect and need a balanced provision for life, including leisure.'[3] If leisure is growing, its contribution to the quality of life, and the problem of leisure in so far as this contribution falls short of its potential, can only increase in importance.

The Sports Council has a vested interest in arguing the importance of leisure. We all have a vested interest in the Sports Council. It is spending our money. So are the Arts Council, the Countryside Commission, the tourist boards and broadcasting authorities. Likewise the local government departments catering for recreation with parks, playing fields, libraries, zoos, museums and other facilities. Leisure has become big business, much of it in the public sector. Few British readers will be familiar with the phrase 'leisure services'. This will change. Leisure is becoming a fully fledged branch of our Welfare State. Are we obtaining value for money? Those sceptical of leisure's importance will rise to this question.

Most writing on leisure lays no claim to scientific status. Until the 1950s British social science itself was little more than a cottage industry, and its pioneers gave their main attention to the apparently more urgent problems of poverty, health, unemployment and housing. Historians charted political and economic developments, while saying little about the people's pastimes. But during the last 25 years an expanding army of academics seeking new outlets for their originality, coupled with a growing awareness of the subject's importance, has led historians, political scientists, geographers, psychologists and sociologists to apply their disciplines' methods to leisure. Until the 1960s a social science of leisure was little more than an aspiration. In the meantime it has become a thriving academic business. A *Directory of Leisure Scholars and Research*[4] compiled at Salford University contains over 500 entries, and Britain now has a flourishing *Leisure Studies Association* which acts as a forum for researchers and practitioners to share ideas, problems and findings. In North American colleges, 40 000 students are pursuing leisure studies,[5] and Britain appears set to follow suit. Loughborough University offers a qualification in recreation management. Since 1978 Salford University has hosted a Centre for Leisure Studies and Research. The Tourism and Recreation Research Unit at Edinburgh, and the Centre for Urban and Regional Studies at Birmingham University now have proven track records in leisure studies. In 1979 a degree course in sports studies, jointly launched by the Newcastle and Sunderland Polytechnics, attracted over 2900 enquiries before commencing. Sheffield Polytechnic followed with a similar programme in 1980. As the following chapters will describe, these academic developments reflect the rise of leisure, the growth of the leisure industries and the expansion of employment in this area.

Few definite conclusions have yet emerged from leisure research advising 'what to do' in order to maximise leisure's contribution to the good life Researchers have confirmed commonsense in demonstrating that leisure facilities *may* contribute to well-being. But they have also shown that this may not happen. There is some rather embarrassing evidence that the leisure services offered by central and local government do little to enhance the lives of many citizens.[6] Researchers, needless to say, remain undeterred by ambiguous findings. They have been further motivated to discover ways of creating a better fit between people's interests and leisure facilities, and an aim of this book is to show how sociology can contribute.

The return of mass unemployment since the mid-1970s has helped to make leisure a topical issue. Lifetime is being shed from work. Lengthening dole queues draw attention to this fact, but the trend is not new. It has been underway since the nineteenth century, which is why there is no excuse for speculating wildly about the future, and acting on the blind faith that expanding our present stock of recreational facilities will resolve the predicaments of the unemployed. Sociology can explain the circumstances under which time released from work becomes leisure. It can supply a knowledge base to assess whether public welfare will be served by further investment in the leisure services. As yet the subject offers no blueprint for happiness. But it can clarify the options, distinguish the futures we may create for ourselves by accident or design and thereby increase the likelihood that we will construct futures we welcome, not those we would have preferred to avoid.

As individuals, social scientists lay no claim to value freedom, but the majority nevertheless attempt to ground their statements in systematically assembled evidence, and to disentangle matters of fact from judgements of value. As a result, social science has enhanced the quality of debate if not, as yet, the quality of leisure itself. Economists have begun to examine the role of leisure in the economy, and to measure the costs and benefits of different leisure facilities. Psychologists are exploring how leisure activities result from and sometimes influence individuals' interests, values, motives and psychic welfare. Geographers' main interest lies in the relationship between land and leisure; they measure the impact of recreational demand on countryside and townscapes, and the connections between physical location and the public's propensity to participate. Political scientists examine the public leisure services and endeavour to clarify objectives, assess results and thereby improve performance.

Sociology's prime interest lies in the role of leisure in society. Why do people in different societies use leisure in different ways? How and why do other social divisions such as those based on age, gender, occupation and education lead to different uses of leisure? In what ways and to what extent do uses of leisure influence behaviour in other spheres of life? Like other social scientists, sociologists normally aspire to establish truths independently of value judgements. But they inevitably become involved in debates about standards, tastes and policies if only because the values that others seek to promote during or through leisure are part of the social reality that sociology explores. Irrespective of their own values, sociologists find themselves informing those who seek to promote sport and the arts 'for their own sake', to preserve standards or to take the cultural heritage to the millions, that the standards they are protecting are not eternal but reflect specific social conditions and interests. Those seeking to assist all members of the public to express and act upon their own interests, whatever these might be, find sociology deflating their pretensions by showing that individuals' conceptions of their interests often reflect not their own natures but the influence of parents, friends and, sometimes, the persuasion industries.

Even if academic social scientists had remained uninterested there would be no shortage of information about the public's uses of leisure. We have mountains of data on how leisure is spent, very little of it collected primarily for social scientists' purposes. During the last 20 years a series of national and regional surveys has furnished information about people's activities.[7] In addition recreational behaviour has been monitored in the General Household Survey.[8] Public providers including the Sports Council, the Countryside Commission, the tourist boards and local authorities have sponsored enquiries to probe the character of their clients and identify likely trends. The mass media chart their audiences diligently; their life-blood, advertising revenue, is at stake. From these enquiries we know a great deal about 'who does what'. We know the proportions of the population that participate in virtually every recreation, and breakdowns are normally available by age, sex, occupational status, income, educational level and car ownership. We know who takes part in which sports, attends the theatre, watches which television programmes and reads which publications. There is a huge quantity of data for leisure scholars to analyse. We are not starved of facts. The main problem is not a shortage of basic information but how to interpret the evidence and decide what the statistics mean.

Sociology's standard complaint is that, having been produced primarily at the behest of the leisure industries with their own problems in mind, the data often fail to address questions that sociologists want to pose. The prime interest of the leisure industries has been to chart present and future markets. The research consequently tells us a great deal about who does what, but little about participants' intentions and gratifications. The 1978 report of a Working Party jointly assembled by the Social Science Research Council and the Sports Council to assess the state of leisure and recreation research draws attention to our lack of knowledge about values, needs, motivations and satisfactions.[9] Despite its size, the leisure data mountain does not take us very far towards understanding the sources and consequences of different uses of leisure. The leisure industries have commissioned research designed to deliver quick and useful results. Providers of sports and other recreation facilities have required information about who benefits, and have sought guidance on the numbers likely to use proposed ventures. There has been less support for the kind of research where the applications would be uncertain and, at best, longer-term. Academic investigators have posed more 'fundamental' questions about the role of leisure, but their efforts have been fragmented. Isolated scholars have produced ideas and mounted 'pilot' studies, but have possessed neither the resources nor organisation for sustained theory-building.

There remain many glaring gaps in our knowledge. We have few detailed observational studies to tell us what actually happens in sports centres, bingo halls and when people trip to the countryside. We know the precise proportions of different age groups who do all these things, but much less about whatever the 'doing' might be. And as already mentioned, the satisfactions people are seeking and deriving remain virtually unexplored.

Mainstream recreation research has assisted the providers of leisure services in addressing their managerial problems, such as the size of the catchment areas needed to support various sports facilities. But the research is less informative when broader *policy* issues are raised. How will the quality of life be enhanced if we invest in arts centres, community halls or sports complexes? How will the benefits compare with those obtainable from investment in public housing, broadcasting or education?

Another unsurprising shortcoming, given that so much of the existing research has been provider-sponsored, concerns its failure to examine the leisure industries themselves from a genuinely critical perspective. Intellectuals' hostility towards popular culture and its transmitters has rarely penetrated leisure research except in the fields of broadcasting and publishing. Apparently value-free surveys have paraded the assumption that if people are interested in any activity they will seek to pursue it, and that facilities will be provided by some branch of the leisure industries. These assumptions ignore the unequal distribution of

power in society, and interrelationships between the leisure
industries and this power structure. The 'politics of leisure' still
awaits an author.

Rather than just *more* research, the study of leisure requires
better enquiries. Among other things, the subject needs the kind
of conceptual and theoretical input that a healthy sociology of
leisure will deliver. The remaining pages seek to prove this
point. They are a statement of what the sociology of leisure
currently has to say – the theories it can offer and the evidence it
has already unearthed. But rather than seeking applause for
momentous accomplishments, this book is more an agenda of
issues about leisure that sociology to date has merely opened.
The matter for immediate decision is whether the questions
deserve further exploration. The following chapters will make
the case for an affirmative answer.

Having staked sociology's interest in its study, the next
chapter tackles the meaning of leisure. As will become apparent,
asking 'What is leisure?' is an introduction to a continuing
debate. There are short, snappy answers on offer – too many for
any one definition to be accepted uncritically, and Chapter 2 will
not supply a 'final' definition. The meaning of leisure is a theme
to be explored throughout this volume, and one of the overall
arguments will be that since leisure is shaped by society, its
character is inevitably modified by wider social changes, which
is why the quest for one eternal definition is pointless. Chapters
2, 3 and 4 present 'background' information about the
development of leisure since the nineteenth century and its
contemporary uses. They describe how leisure was reshaped
following the Industrial Revolution, its subsequent growth, how
our pastimes have changed, and conclude by portraying
contemporary Britain at play. Apart from being basic and
essential data, presenting the 'facts and figures' will serve a
broader purpose; it will illustrate why sociology insists that we
need to know more than 'who does what' in order to understand
and explain leisure behaviour fully. Chapters 5 and 6 examine
relationships between uses of leisure and individuals' other social
roles, at work and in the family, the main topics that empirical
sociological research has explored. The evidence will demonstrate the many ways in which leisure 'reflects' the wider society,

but these chapters also present the arguments of researchers who have been impressed by the autonomy of leisure, the extent to which its uses are independent of individuals' other social statuses, and the ways in which leisure itself can influence our attitudes and behaviour in other spheres. Chapter 7 returns to historical trends and the likely role of leisure in the future. It juxtaposes theories which suggest that the end of the industrial era is in sight, and that we are on the threshold of a 'society of leisure', against forecasts which envisage perhaps modest growth but little change in leisure's role. The concluding chapter deals with the leisure industries, particularly the public sector, and the leisure policies, actual and potential, that direct its activities. This chapter focuses on whether we need a full-blooded government policy and programme for leisure. Like social scientists, politicians may be well advised to take leisure seriously, but how strenuously do we want them to pursue this interest?

Overall the volume aims to show that the sociology of leisure can offer more than tables enumerating the types of people who engage in different activities. It aims to demonstrate how studying the sources and consequences of leisure behaviour can shed light on broader forces and currents of change, and chart the futures that, either by choice or default, we will create for ourselves. Sociologists' professional interest in their own societies, present and future, explains their concern for leisure. A much wider public has an equally vested interest in the debates that the sociology of leisure can open.

2

LEISURE AND INDUSTRIALISM

Leisure time, activity and experience

An introduction to sociology is an invitation to a series of
debates rather than the presentation of an agreed body of
knowledge. Those acquainted with the discipline will have been
unsurprised to learn that even leisure's definition is controversial. In this case, however, sociology's theoretical chaos is not
entirely to blame. As already suggested, leisure's character has
varied according to time and place. Furthermore, even hoping
for a historically specific definition that will enable us all to
pinpoint the relevant parts of our contemporary lives is chasing a
daydream. It is not difficult to *compose* crystal-clear definitions of
leisure: there are many on offer. The problem lies in
operationalising any clear definition. Linguistic precision flounders when faced with people's untidy lives. Most of us can name
occasions, maybe when gardening, repairing our cars or visiting
relatives, when we feel that our behaviour is partly leisure,
partly something else. Leisure has no precise boundaries; a fact
of life which no conjuring with words will change.

The dozens of verbal formulae can be grouped into two main
approaches to leisure's definition. The first, sometimes called
'residual' definitions, treat leisure as a *part of life*. These
concepts of leisure can be further divided according to whether
leisure is distinguished from other spheres in terms of time,
activity, experience or some combination of all three. Time
definitions treat leisure as the residue left when work and other
physically necessary acts, such as eating and sleeping, and social
obligations such as housework, have been discharged. Leisure is
conceived as *spare or free time* in which we can please ourselves;

the part of life that remains when we have fulfilled our duties, the time of our own to use as we please.

✻ ˒ When leisure is defined as a type of activity, *play* features as the central concept. Play's essential character lies in its separation from 'ordinary' life, a separation marked by some combination of rules, time and place.[1] We play games, a process known as recreation. Since it is 'only a game' the result does not really matter, meaning that the consequences can be contained and need not intrude into our political, working and family lives. Needless to say, many people take their games very seriously. Is it possible to enjoy any game fully without participating whole-heartedly? Yet however serious our commitment, play involves stepping outside our normal routines, and our normal 'selves'. It enables us to express and develop aspects of our characters that would otherwise remain hidden. During play we can 'try out' new roles and personas. Play can be educational in the broadest meaning of the term, for children and for adults.

Definitions that treat leisure as a type of experience say that it is *intrinsically pleasant and fulfilling*, and therefore contains its own reward. Academic writers have attempted to sharpen this common-sense phrasing. Work can be defined to refer to a broader category of activities than paid employment, to encompass all actions on nature, people and ideas that increase their value for future use. In addition to paid employment, housework and educational work fall within this definition. The opposite of work, thus defined, is *consumption*, when we 'use up' resources. Consumption is self-justifying. It is *expressive* behaviour rather than calculated to further a longer-term objective, and cannot be identified in terms of any external, objective characteristics. Gardening may be practised for its own sake, to sell the vegetable produce or to enjoy the eventual sight of the flower-beds. It is the experience of the actor that is crucial, and leisure can be defined accordingly.

Scholars have conjured with various combinations of time, activity and experience in their attempts to define leisure. Definitions intended for use in survey research normally discount experience, since this leisure concept is so difficult, maybe impossible, to operationalise. For practical purposes, leisure research has been the study of the games people play during free time. If nothing else, this is probably an adequate starting point. Sociology does not dismiss this concept of leisure. But a comparative sociological perspective demonstrates that this type of residual definition is more appropriate in some societies than others. It is a useful approach to understanding leisure in *industrial* societies, where time, activity and experience can be treated as the basic *elements* of leisure. In everyday life the elements *tend* to coexist, but not always, which is why certain times, activities and experiences are felt to be only partly leisure. To appreciate how industrial man's leisure is 'lived', the essential point to grasp is that in everyday life the elements are normally interwoven. It is unnecessary to disentangle the elements to enjoy leisure, only to understand it.

Leisure as a way of life

Definitions which treat leisure as 'parts' of life, irrespective of their emphases within the time, activity and experience trilogy, discount an older, alternative, and in some ways more appealing concept that can be traced to the ancient Greeks. Rather than any special times, activities or experiences, the Greeks treated leisure as a *quality of life* in general. The term stood for a humane ideal, the state attained by the 'whole man' who had developed all aspects of his character and the widest possible range of interests. Education was oriented towards this ideal, as were the original Olympic Games. They were religious and artistic in addition to sporting festivals. Athletic ability was believed to indicate divine power, but the competitor who was able to excel in only one event was considered a perversion of the true Olympic spirit.[2] In classical Greece it was believed that the ideal, balanced way of life was incompatible with work, which was therefore left to slaves. Indeed, a major justification of slavery in the ancient world alleged its necessity if free men were to lead lives of leisure.

Later in European history, especially with the rise of Puritanism, work in one's vocation or calling came to be regarded as an essential aspect of religious and self-expression,[3] but the Greek notion of leisure was retained virtually intact. And this older concept of leisure is still in use today. It is wielded by critics of popular culture and contemporary forms of play which are condemned as pointless, confined within useless fragments of spare time, and ruthlessly exploited by commercial interests.[4] It is also employed by critics of residual definitions who insist that leisure is still better treated as a ubiquitous process or quality of life in general.

Who is right? As anticipated in the previous chapter, my own view is that there is no single 'correct' definition, and that the nature of leisure has varied depending on the character of the surrounding society. Leisure has not been an unchanging entity, varying only in the amounts people have possessed, and how it has been used. The meaning of leisure has been rescripted by history. It was transformed during the Industrial Revolution, and it is necessary to appreciate that at one time leisure can be a pervasive quality of life, at another just a part, both to grasp the impact of industrialism, and to understand how alleged trends towards a post-industrial society may once again rescript the meaning of leisure.

Work and leisure in industrial society

The Industrial Revolution which separates us from the ancient Greeks, medieval courtiers and rustic village life was much more than an economic affair. A new way of life and a distinctive type of leisure were born. Everyone recognises many continuities between pre-industrial and modern society. Fun, amusement, excitement, self-expression – all the experiences derived from modern leisure have a history as old as humanity. Non-working time and play also pre-date industrialism. Nevertheless, industrialism forged a distinctive package. All the elements of industrial leisure can be regarded as ubiquitous aspects of social and human reality,[5] but prior to industrialism they were diffused throughout life in general, not parcelled together.

Pre-industrial man had plenty of time for play. In medieval Europe over 100 saints' and feast days were recognised. Notwithstanding the influence of Puritanism, in 1761 the Bank of England still closed on 47 bank holidays. Play is not a recent invention, but in pre-industrial Britain, recreation was thoroughly blended into community life, inseparable from family, religion and work. Feast days were not just holidays, they were also holy days. Individuals played among fellow workers and neighbours. Leisure was a pervasive aspect of their way of life, and the 'leisure class' consisted not of idle folk whose lives were work-free, but individuals who were able to lead the 'full life' which extended all aspects of their characters. Peasants were less likely to attain this ideal than courtiers, but it remained relevant to their existence. It was 'the seasonal rhythms of agriculture and the celebrating of the ecclesiastical calendar which together provided the framework for recreational customs'.[6] Popular sports like hunting were rooted in economic activity. Others including tournaments and archery served as military training. It is meaningless to ask whether industrial man enjoys more leisure than his ancestors. He possesses a different type of leisure which defies quantitative comparison with the play of earlier eras. The latter was too thoroughly woven into work, family, community life and religious festivals to allow anyone to ask exactly how much leisure time people possessed, and how much expenditure was devoted to recreation. This traditional way of life was destroyed as the industrial age dawned.

Industrialisation uprooted villagers, transported them to towns and factories, and, in the process, destroyed many traditional recreations. Most important of all, industrialism introduced new ways of allocating time and perceptions of work. Employment became a compartment of life. Work became the sale of labour power for agreed units of time during which individuals were subject to the discipline of employers and machinery. Only when work has been industrialised do we encounter 'residual' leisure – time that is free for play, when the individual can not only 'please' himself but 'be' himself. In industry people work specified hours in special work organisations (offices and factories), and are subject to the authority of machines and bosses whose writ ends with the close of each working day, at the factory gates, and it is this organisation of work that creates leisure as a corner of life where we can be our own masters. Because it compartmentalises work, industrialism inevitably transforms leisure into a part of life. This is why, in industrial societies, work and leisure have been such an inseparable couplet. Intellectuals have found themselves unable to describe the character of leisure without using work as a yardstick. And for identical reasons, it is arguable that members of the public have been unable to experience leisure unless work has also been part of their lives. Holidays depend on there being work-days, just as the experience of the weekend is contingent on a work-week.

The destruction of the older way of life was not entirely by the impersonal forces of industrialism and urbanisation. The 'powers that be' consciously sought to erase the depravity and coarseness of popular recreation. 'Moralists and reformers, those least hesitant of writers, have seldom been fully satisfied with the character or consequences of the people's pastimes.'[7] Concern for the quality of popular culture has been endemic throughout history, but during the nineteenth century moral considerations were backed by economic interests. 'Underlying much of the growing hostility towards popular recreation was the concern for effective labour discipline.'[8] 'Green' labour had to be welded into the factory system. Labourers who were accustomed to a different rhythm of life had to be disciplined into industriousness. Complaints about poor time-keeping, drunkenness and lack of effort abounded. Manufacturers had long deplored the people's playfulness. In 1776 Joseph Wedgewood had complained, 'Our men here have been at play four days this week, it being Burslem Wakes. I have rough'd and smoothed them over, and promised them a long Christmas, but I know it is all in vain, for Wakes must be observed as though the world was to end with them.'[9] Previously, in 1670, Thomas Munn had attributed Britain's weakened trading position to 'the general leprosy of our piping, potting, feasting factions and misspending of our time in idleness and pleasure.'[10] Industrial employers demanded long hours of work, by pre-industrial as well as modern standards, at jobs which often required strenuous effort and offered little intrinsic satisfaction, and the Industrial Revolution was accomplished only because, in the nineteenth century, these demands were successfully imposed.

This was the background to the nineteenth-century campaigns for temperance and mass schooling, and moral assaults on idleness. By 1834 the Bank of England recognised only four bank holidays. The Puritan praise of work was revived with a vengeance. Popular recreations such as cock-fighting and bull-baiting were suppressed, though the gentry's field sports remained untouched. Their pastimes did not threaten industrial discipline. Recreation reached a low ebb during the second quarter of the nineteenth century. Not only traditional pastimes, an entire way of life was lost, and the new industrial cities incorporated few recreational facilities.[11]

When recreation was revived, a story told in Chapter 3, it was as part of a new kind of leisure, itself a product of the logic of industrialism which transformed the entire pattern of everyday life. The rationality of work in industry, imposed by technology and bureaucracy, means that, for most workers, consumption and expressive behaviour offering pleasant, fulfilling experiences have to be channelled principally through play, in free time. Hence the tendency, though it has never been more than a powerful tendency, for time, activity and experiential elements to coalesce making leisure in industrial society a part of life rather than a quality of life in general. Industrialism involves a division of labour not only in industry itself, but throughout society. It involves the creation of specialist institutions dealing, for example, with health and education, and leisure. It is only when leisure has become a part of life that specifically leisure organisations, entire leisure industries, can be born, and that ideas about play, sport and art for their own sake can take root. Before the Industrial Revolution the thought rarely occurred that politics and religion might be kept out of art and sport; they were so obviously and inextricably interwoven.

Leisure as a part of life was not completely unknown prior to industrialism. In the ancient world, even before the rise of the Roman Empire, the connection between religion and athletics became as tenuous as between modern soccer fixtures and Easter.[12] Athletics became a professional occupation and a mass entertainment. Purists deplored the passing of the true Olympic spirit. Like contemporary politicians, Roman emperors were aware of the value of feeding the masses with spectacles – with circuses in addition to bread. They understood how their prestige could be enhanced by appearing at popular sporting events. The pay-off from sports sponsorship was well known to the Romans. But this form of leisure was lost with the decay of Roman civilisation. Play and amusement sank back into the rhythms of agriculture, church and community life, to rise afresh only with the Industrial Revolution.

The contemporary role of leisure

To understand leisure in present-day Britain, must we concern ourselves with the Industrial Revolution? One conclusion of general theoretical importance, and therefore of contemporary relevance, is that leisure's character has always been stamped by the surrounding social order. This is one reason why a sociological perspective is indispensable for a proper understanding of the subject. But the main contemporary relevance of the impact of industrialism hinges around the controversy as to whether we are still living in an industrial society.

There is no fundamental dispute among historians and sociologists that the Industrial Revolution destroyed a traditional, rural way of life into which recreation was blended, and created a new type of leisure. Nor is there any dispute about the long-term growth of leisure since the advent of industrialism. There are arguments about its pace and implications, but no one disputes that today, on average, we possess more leisure than our great-grandparents. We have more time free from work, and more money to spend on recreation. Where the arguments arise is over whether this growth has been part of a configuration of social structural changes during which the character of leisure, its role in people's lives and society at large, have been transformed in such a way as to render obsolete our now orthodox definitions.

Some writers allege that the growth of leisure has spread ripple effects throughout the wider society. It is argued that the values associated with play and leisure time, pleasing oneself and having fun, are becoming increasingly central to the ethos of our 'post-industrial civilisation'. As leisure becomes big business served by its own leisure industries, the argument runs, the latter become increasingly important architects of the culture of society at large. As this happens, it is alleged, individuals begin to use leisure interests and activities not only to fill spare time, but as sources of their most basic values and foundations for their social and self-identities. People's ideas about their own and their fellows' characters are said to be determined increasingly by how they play rather than how they work. This line of reasoning hints that leisure may have outgrown the niche defined during the creation of industrial society, that leisure is now becoming much more than a residual element squeezed from the economy. Leisure is seen as a growing force whose influence now extends into multiple spheres. In its most extreme form, the argument claims that leisure is becoming the pivotal process, and that we are now on the verge of a society of leisure. Whether industrial society has really been superseded, and the likely advent of this society of leisure, will be fully discussed in Chapter 7. The matter of immediate concern is this: has leisure's role changed to such an extent that the subject has outgrown residual definitions? Has leisure outstripped the time/activity/ experience package that was forged with the Industrial Revolution? Is it still appropriate to define leisure as a residual sphere devoted to play?

Writers who argue that leisure values and interests are now invading and helping to restructure other areas of life believe that the residual concept needs to be abandoned or at least complemented. According to Neulinger, 'The traditional sociological, residual definition of leisure as time left over is slowly being replaced or at least supplemented by a psychological one, that identifies leisure as a state of mind. Such a metamorphosis is a slow and gradual process coming about because the condition of society and the problems confronting us in the post-industrial era demand it.'[13] Rather than simply researching how individuals spend their free time, Murphy has advised investigators to pay greater attention to individuals' attempts to be 'at leisure', efforts which need not be confined to free time, or channelled through games.[14] Is it any longer sufficient for researchers to probe the extent and ways in which individuals' domestic and work roles affect their leisure behaviour? Do we now also need to explore the extent to which work and domestic life have become leisurely? These questions are of more than academic interest. If leisure is becoming more of a pervasive quality than merely a part of life, catering for any growth of leisure by enlarging specifically leisure industries and services may not be the most appropriate response.

How to cater for leisure cannot be finally settled 'by definition'. Rather than leading to a definite conclusion, discussing the concept of leisure can achieve no more than opening a field for debate. Researchers must inevitably disagree on the definition of leisure. The quest for an eternal, universally valid concept is mistaken. Sociology can keep us clear of this blind alley. Analysts must forever seek to improve and sharpen concepts to enhance our understanding 'of how leisure is influenced by and, in turn, how it may influence the surrounding society. If the role of leisure is changing, if leisure is ceasing to be a product of industrialism's logic and becoming a force shaping individuals' broader life-styles, then our definitions through which leisure is addressed will need to change accordingly. If leisure is no longer imprisoned in a residual sphere of life, if individuals are increasingly able to use the resources unleashed by leisure to reshape their entire life-styles, history will have turned full circle. As in ancient Greece, leisure will once again have become a quality of life in general, but for more than a small, privileged stratum of free men.

3

THE GROWTH OF LEISURE

Proclamations of leisure's growth have a history as old as industrialism. Commentators began to debate the implications in the closing decades of the nineteenth century. During the inter-war years it was argued that, '. . . all the forces at work are combining to shift the main centre of the worker's life more and more from his daily work to his daily leisure'.[1] This remark has been echoed by numerous subsequent writers.

The containment of work

The long-term growth of leisure is a product of two principal trends. Firstly, it results from containing the demands of work upon life-time. Prior to the nineteenth century, in manufacturing, a 10-hour working day, between 6.00 a.m. and 6.00 p.m., was customary. The Industrial Revolution saw some employers, notably in textiles, attempting to impose even longer hours, and early trade union struggles aimed to protect the 10-hour day in addition to members' earnings. By the mid-nineteenth century, normal hours of work were 10 per day, 6 days each week, with no paid vacations. Women and children, in addition to men, were subjected to this regime. Subsequently, however, the story is not of customary hours being defended, but of life-time being progressively released from work.

Unlike the growth of wages and salaries, gains in free time have not been slow and steady. The work-week in industry has been trimmed through a series of widely spaced steps.[2] Basic hours of work were reduced in the 1870s; after the First World War; again after the Second World War; then during the 1960s.

Shorter hours have always been a standard trade union demand, but employers have never relished the prospect of machines standing idle, or paying overtime premiums, and have resisted these claims more strenuously than pressure for higher wages. A shorter work-week has been conceded only under exceptional conditions: when trade unions' bargaining power has been enhanced by full employment, but when the unions have simultaneously feared a growth of unemployment.

Actual hours worked have not always followed trends in the basic work-week. Between the 1940s and the 1970s, overtime working flourished as basic hours fell. Moonlighting, taking a second job, also became prevalent. Estimates of the numbers involved range from 1 to 3 million. The Inland Revenue reckons that over 7 per cent of all economic activity now occurs in an informal or 'black', tax-free economy. During the 1950s, 60s and 70s hours of work have not plummeted, but we could be on the threshold of another plunge in the now customary work-week. By the end of the nineteenth century, the five-and-a-half-day week had become the norm. Spectator sports were among the beneficiaries. Since the Second World War a five-day week has been standard. Long plateaux are not unprecedented, and likewise any future movement towards a four-day work-week will not be without historical parallel.

Leisure time has increased not only through trimming the work-week but also as a result of the establishment and subsequent enlargement of holiday entitlement. By the end of the nineteenth century industrialists were recognising Wakes Weeks. Annual holidays, though still without pay for manual workers, had become the norm. During the 1930s two weeks with pay plus public holidays became usual. Today three and four weeks have become standard. The demands of work have been further contained by completely releasing certain sections of the population from the work-force. Child labour has been relegated to history books. Even adolescent employment is now becoming uncommon. The creation of statutory and voluntary pension schemes has encouraged the institutionalisation of retirement.

These trends have not benefited all individuals in all oc-

cupations. In some managerial and professional jobs, there has
been no decline in weekly hours of work since the beginning of
the century.[3] Professions like medicine, the law and university
teaching have been transformed from gentlemanly ways of life
into real occupations. There are some jobs including teaching
and the Civil Service where holiday entitlement has not
increased since the Second World War. Rather than their lives
being freed from work, the trend has been towards more
married women taking jobs outside their homes. The growth of
non-working time has not been evenly spread, and for those who
have benefited the pace of change has been gradual rather than
cataclysmic. Few people will ever have felt engulfed by spare
time as a result of this trend. But the overall direction of change
has been unmistakable, and is continuing. Time–budget data
show that between 1961 and 1975 the amount of leisure time at
the public's disposal grew by 18 per cent.[4] Over generations the
gains have been much more substantial. Today we enjoy
considerably more non-working time than our nineteenth-
century forebears.

Rising incomes

The second long-term trend responsible for unleashing leisure
has been the spread of prosperity. Once again, this trend is
anything but recent in origin. Speculation about the likely
embourgeoisement of an affluent proletariat can be traced to the
1870s. Rising wage levels were then enabling more workers to
buy their own houses and take holidays away from home. In the
nineteenth century, as today, these were taken as signs of
'respectability'. Since 1900 the real per capita value of our Gross
National Product has tripled. Standards of living have not
risen steadily from year to year, but the long-term trend is
unmistakable. Even during the 'depressed' inter-war years, for
those who remained in employment, the growth of prosperity
continued. The middle classes pioneered motoring and flying as
leisure activities, while the public in general adopted the radio
and cinema.[5]

Spending on recreation is income-elastic: people with the

higher incomes devote the greater proportions to leisure goods and services, and as the general standard of living rises, so does leisure's share of consumer spending.[6] During the 1950s over two-thirds of households became equipped with televisions. The 1960s saw the family motor car send a wave of leisure across the countryside. The tourist trades flourished, and during the 1970s a public with cash to spare for the necessary equipment inspired a boom in participant sport.

Like non-working time, prosperity remains far from evenly spread. During the 1950s poverty was rediscovered in the heart of the so-called affluent society. Critics protested that the tail lagged as far as ever behind the average household's income. Progressive income taxes and the Welfare State had achieved no more than a shift of resources from the extremely wealthy to others on above-average incomes, and this remains true today. But the overall standard of living has nevertheless risen. Those still defined as 'in poverty' are not struggling beneath the subsistence level featured in pre-1939 poverty surveys. They have shared the overall rise in prosperity. Some are still denied the leisure opportunities that others can take for granted. Relative poverty and low pay are persistent problems. Every year trade union negotiators are able to ask the nation how local authority manual workers, hospital ancillaries and others on low basic wages can be expected to provide their families with decent living standards. The economic circumstances of the retired, the chronically sick and others entirely dependent on state benefits still arouse concern. Eight per cent of all households today are single-parent families, mostly headed by women, and their life-styles are rarely affluent. Many of the 20 per cent of all families where a man and woman endeavour to support themselves and dependent children on a single wage or salary are anything but prosperous. But well over a half of all married owmen are now breadwinners. Many families enjoy dual incomes, and some of these contain no dependants. Neither leisure time nor income are distributed equally. Many households are unable to afford motor transport and holidays abroad. But on average today we possess not only more leisure time, but much greater spending power than our grandparents, and many of us enjoy a great deal of each.

Demographic change

There is a third historical trend, demographic change, that has interacted with rising living standards and the containment of working time to accentuate leisure's growth. Since the nineteenth century birth and death-rates have fallen. People live longer and have fewer children. The consequent decline in the proportion of children in the population has enabled the young to be supported more generously than formerly. Educational opportunities have widened. Affluent parents with small families are able to 'spoil' teenage children.[7] Those proceeding to higher education are now guaranteed (means-tested) maintenance grants. Since the 1950s, teenagers who join the work-force, with their minimal domestic responsibilities, have also joined the big spenders and been courted by the leisure industries.

The decline in mortality has meant a rise in the proportion of elderly people in the population, and their support is a growing problem. Retirement as a normal phase in the life-cycle is a twentieth-century phenomenon. Whether this phase of life when individuals are released from work, and also, in many cases, from family obligations, can be described as leisure is a controversial issue. Many retired people possess neither the health nor the income to exploit recreational opportunities. Excess time can hang heavily when not mixed with physical and economic power. But the declining death-rate, coupled with the fall in fertility, has freed the majority of adults from child-rearing responsibilities well before the age of retirement. The typical woman now has her youngest child in school when in her early thirties. The small, planned family, household gadgets and convenience foods have released women from the routines of child-bearing, child-rearing, mending, washing, cooking and darning that once made housework a full-time occupation interrupted only by death. The majority of women have exploited this situation by returning to the labour force rather than opting for gracious idleness, but the fact remains that demographic trends have created space in the life-cycle that did not previously exist, particularly during youth and the post-parental phase, when many individuals now have time and money for leisure on a historically unprecedented scale.

The growth of recreation

Given the manner in which industrialism created leisure as a
part of life by fusing free time, consumption and opportunities
to play, the growth of recreation can be regarded as a natural
corollary of the containment of working time and the spread of
affluence. In recent years the growing popularity of participant
sport, active outdoor recreation and alcohol have attracted
widespread comment. What is sometimes overlooked is that
rather than completely novel developments, these trends are but
the latest instalments in a saga that began in the nineteenth
century when reductions in working hours and the growth of
real incomes first laid the foundations for a rebirth of popular
culture.

Many older pastimes were lost as industrialism disrupted
traditional ways of life. Some recreations were deliberately
supressed by moralists and employers who were seeking to
cultivate a disciplined work-force. But after the 1850s, instead of
repressing the people's pastimes, the middle classes began to
promote worthwhile, edifying, rational, temperate recreations.[8]
All our modern leisure industries have their origins in this
period. Public provision began when municipalities laid out
parks and open spaces, built libraries and baths. Present-day
local authority departments under leisure, recreation and similar
titles have grown from these foundations. In the nineteenth
century the aim was clearly broadcast; to spread civilised
life-styles that would help to resolve the 'social question', the
condition of the urban mass, by spreading morality and culture.[9]

The voluntary, non-statutory, non-profit-making sector of the
leisure industries also has nineteenth-century origins. The sports
associations that wrote the laws and organised competitions
served as prototypes for many other voluntary bodies. Sports
including soccer were devised by and for middle-class males in
public schools and universities, then taken to the masses, often
with missionary zeal, via churches, schools and youth
organisations. It was believed that sport nurtured both health
and character, and a desire to 'do good' has remained a major
inspiration in voluntary leisure organisations. Hence the
multitude of bodies which aim to service the leisure of groups
with special needs ranging from toddlers in play-groups to the

elderly. But self-help has always been an equally powerful motive in the voluntary sector. Soccer, golf, tennis and stamp-collecting enthusiasts have organised not only to 'do good' for others, but also to pursue their own interests. Before the end of the nineteenth century the working class had learnt the habit. Working men's clubs, brass bands and other recreational institutes joined political organisations and co-operative societies in catering for an array of interests. Sometimes the workers emulated and earned patronage from their 'betters', as in educational institutes and sports clubs. But by the end of the nineteenth century the urban masses had begun to design their own culture, assisted by the third branch of the leisure industries, the commercial sector.

Within the limits of the law, business responds to whatever people want, provided they are able and willing to pay. It services tourists, gamblers and participant sportsmen. It offers music and other forms of entertainment, reading matter, alcohol and tobacco. Nowadays the suppliers range from small shops and catering establishments to multinational conglomerates. Leisure has become big business, built on the relatively modest foundations laid during the nineteenth century.

Recreational habits have subsequently changed, due largely to technological developments that have introduced new forms of communication including television, and transport such as the private motor car. But these developments have all built on foundations cast in the aftermath of the Industrial Revolution. As far as leisure is concerned, the nineteenth century was a far more innovative era than our present time. It achieved a revolution in forms of recreation. Many traditional pastimes such as drinking were retained, and most modern sports have ancestries that can be traced to antiquity, but their organisation was completely overhauled in the nineteenth century. They became tuned to the rhythm of industrial life, part of the new leisure industries. Subsequently there have been no comparable revolutions in the organisation of leisure.

The street culture

From the 1870s, recreational habits with roots in the emergent culture of the urban working classes became increasingly evident. Sports clubs, brass bands, choirs and working men's clubs blossomed as 'working-class communities' arose from disorganised squalor. A feature of the recreations fashioned by the urban masses was their roots in the culture of the street, the unrivalled centre for working class social life, and the local community still remains a focus for a great deal of working-class leisure. During the twentieth century urban redevelopment and other social changes have undermined many older communities. The rise of the mass leisure industries has also diminished the neighbourhood's former importance. But in many parts of Britain, street-corner and doorstep sociability, local working men's clubs and pubs, darts, domino and football leagues are preserving uses of evenings and weekends that were fashioned a century ago.

Victorian streets were lively places.[10] Besides transport they hosted commerce, bands, donkey rides, and Punch and Judy shows. Above all, they were venues for sociability. Spectacles such as fires and hangings attracted huge crowds. Sports associations, Sunday schools and working men's clubs all drew strength from the neighbourliness that was to become a hallmark of the working-class community, and commercial recreation was similarly grafted on to the street culture. Song, supper, concert rooms and variety saloons offered various combinations of food, drink and entertainment, from which the 'pub' and music-hall eventually evolved. Until the closing decades of the century theatres were bawdy, lustful places. They became respectable only during a process of differentiation when the theatre, as distinct from the music-hall, segregated drinking from variety performances and heeded reformers' concern for safety and cleanliness.

Another adjunct to the street was the commercial pleasure garden offering food, drink, dancing, fireworks, animal displays, tight-rope and other performances. Travelling fairs enjoyed their heyday around the turn of the century.[11] The fair was a traditional institution with deep roots in medieval society, but during the nineteenth century, in the industrial towns, the fair's commercial functions diminished and entertainment became the prime role. Travelling fairs remain part of the leisure scene in the late twentieth century, and are still operated mainly by the closed intermarrying community of show-business families that travelled Victorian England. They still offer employment to itinerant drop-outs, the gaff lads, but since the First World War, alongside other older recreations, the fairs have been pressured by the rise of additional leisure industries employing technologies that offer access to mass audiences.

Tourism

One form of recreation much favoured by Victorian reformers that truly caught on was the 'outing', subsequently the longer holiday away from home. 'Days out' had a long history, but were formerly restricted to distances that could be travelled on foot, or by horse and cart. The arrival of steamers (the original reason for building piers at seaside resorts) and, after the 1840s, the railways, widened horizons and led to mass invasions of the wealthy's former havens. In 1835 117,000 people travelled to Brighton by stage-coach; in 1862 132,000 arrived by rail on Easter Monday alone.[12] For a later generation the charabanc joined the train as a means of transport, usually to the seaside, but also for excursions to exhibitions and other events.

Formerly the 'grand tour' had been part of the life-style only of the wealthy and great, and until the 1830s seaside resorts catered exclusively for the wealthy. Subsequently they were transformed into mass playgrounds, initially with the full support of the reforming middle classes. Day excursions were organised by firms, charitable societies and Sunday schools. 'Give poor children a happy day' was a favourite motto. The day out was a major occasion. Organisers published itineraries and menus, meals were accompanied by speeches, and everyone wore their 'best'.[13] Since the 1950s the family car has transformed the day out into a common diversion rather than an 'occasion', and by the turn of the century, for many workers, it had already been displaced by the holiday as the highlight of the year.

The seaside had become fashionable during the eighteenth century, taking its rationale from the older spa resorts.[14] Seaside towns then began to rival the inland spas as pleasure, health and social centres. Royal patronage elevated the status of Brighton, and seaside resorts in general. Sea-bathing was credited with remarkable health-giving powers. Sunbathing and suntans, however, did not become fashionable until the 1890s,[15] by which time the seaside holiday had become a mass leisure activity which had no parallel in pre-industrial times. Subsequently holidaymaking habits have changed. People have more disposable time and income. They are able to take longer vacations and venture further afield. But the contemporary holiday remains fundamentally the same leisure activity that was fashioned in Victorian times.

The spread of holidaymaking after the 1870s was based on growing prosperity and reduced hours of work. Progressive employers began recognising Wakes Weeks. Until the 1930s paid holidays, like sick leave, normally remained a white-collar perk, but by the turn of the century it was the standard practice for factories to close for a week or fortnight. In some towns all establishments recognised common holidays, and vacations away from home, like the fair and music hall, became communal occasions. Work-mates and neighbours would travel together. Resorts acquired specific catchment areas, laying habits that continue to this day. The reforming middle classes initially encouraged workers to save for a week by the sea – the epitome of respectability, but by the end of the nineteenth century the resorts had been overwhelmed by the culture of their customers. Commercial enterprises joined charities and employers in organising excursions, amusement parks and slot machines appeared, and the holiday became a time of liberation, of 'letting go'. The gentry retreated to a few remaining fashionable centres such as Cowes, but mainly abroad, with the Riviera as the 'in' destination.

In addition to domestic holidaymaking, the foundations of the international tourist industry were laid in the nineteenth century. In the 1850s Thomas Cook, who was followed by a string of emulators, pioneered the package holiday and thereby opened a new pleasure periphery, an escape from urban uniformity to the exotic. During the twentieth century manual workers have begun venturing to the Riviera and Costa Brava, repeating a historical pattern whereby styles of recreation initially developed by and for the prosperous become aspects of mass leisure. The British pioneered the tourism that has subsequently become big business throughout the world. It now accounts for over 6 per cent of all international trade.[16] The conventional view is that tourism enhances the standards of life not only of tourists, but their hosts as well, who benefit from employment and foreign currency.[17] In recent years, however, attention has been drawn to the damage that tourism can inflict on host economies and cultures.[18] A substantial proportion of the earnings from tourism flows straight out of the host society via airline and tour operators. Within the local economy, benefits are concentrated in limited sectors such as hotels and entertainment. The remainder of the population finds itself bearing the costs of an expensive infrastructure including roads and sewage, and competing for accommodation, including housing, against wealthy visitors. The Welsh, and Londoners, are currently awakening to the costs of successful tourist industries.

Sport

Probably the most spectacular of all developments in recreation during the second half of the nineteenth century was the arrival of modern sports. By the turn of the century the Englishman's sport bore little resemblance to his forefathers' pastimes. One change was the reduction of violence. The ancient riotous game of football where matches were little more than ritualised fights with no written rules or external authority other than local customs, was transformed with laws appropriate for play in urban areas, and consistent with the rhythm of industrial life that required the completion of matches within relatively short time spans.[19] Not only the use of fists but 'hacking' was outlawed early in the history of association football. Most of our present-day sports' rules were devised during this period. The initiative arose in the public schools and universities which produced the players who founded the sporting associations. The law prohibiting 'ungentlemanly conduct' testifies to modern football's social origins. Britain led the world in codifying rules and establishing associations to organise competitions. Hence *the*

Football Association and *the* Amateur Athletics Association have no national prefixes to their titles.

Soccer was initially developed by and for 'gentlemen', but it rapidly caught on among the urban masses, and subsequently throughout the world. The aims of the sport's promoters may have been to teach self-discipline and thereby civilise the lower orders, but soccer's appeal has always rested on other foundations. Apart from being an exciting sport to play and watch, soccer is an ideal street game.[20] Furthermore, participation need not require special equipment. Its appeal as a spectator sport is not unrelated to the fact that so many spectators have played the game themselves. The rise of football as a mass entertainment was facilitated by wider social changes in the closing decades of the nineteenth century; the advent of the five-and-a-half-day week, trams, railways, the telegraph and the creation of a national press. By the end of the century the leading clubs, with semi-professional players, were attracting crowds of modern proportions.

Britons like to believe that throughout the first half of the twentieth century British football led the world, but it was not until after the Second World War that its international strength was fully tested. Throughout the inter-war years the British associations remained outside FIFA (the international governing body) and did not participate in the early World Cups. *The* Football Association was insisting that it should remain the ultimate authority on the laws of the game, and was refusing to compete against countries which had been enemies or neutral during the First World War.[21]

As soccer became the people's game it was dropped by the public schools. There is no necessary reason why soccer should have a mainly working-class appeal. It was entirely a matter of the status and values that became associated with the sport. The mere fact that soccer was adopted by the working class diminished its appeal to gentlemen.[22] The Rugby Union whose amateur ethic coincided with the aristocratic values being assimilated by the rising bourgeoisie, gradually supplanted soccer as the major winter sport in public schools and universities.

The leisure dialectic

One school of thought alleges that the leisure industries that first appeared during the nineteenth century are best understood as apparatuses of social control, and it is certainly true that the urban working class did not fashion new types of recreation entirely from its own resources. Opportunities promoted by the middle classes were influential. Attempts by their 'betters' to influence the masses in 'worthwhile' recreation have a history as old as humanity, but during the nineteenth century these efforts intensified. Following the limited success of attempts to suppress traditional pastimes which were seen as inimical to industrial discipline, the nineteenth-century middle classes embraced the idea of leisure and concentrated on promoting 'rational recreation'.[23] Working-class holidays, initially day excursions, then longer trips away from home, were deliberately promoted by employers as alternatives to fairs, drink and fighting. The seaside was considered less disruptive. Holidaymaking became associated with temperance, saving and self-improvement; in one word, with respectability.[24] Sport was valued and promoted for its character-forming properties. It was hoped that football would nurture qualities of industriousness, team-spirit and self-control. Parks, open spaces and swimming baths were welcomed as means of nurturing healthy workers and soldiers. Leisure was offered to the industrial proletariat as a reward for working. This 'ideology of leisure' offered compensation in the after-hours for any deprivations of the working day. At the same time, the nineteenth century's moral entrepreneurs were aware that leisure could be a threat to industrial discipline. The devil would make work for idle hands and minds. The masses could be tempted by hedonistic values. Hence the need to promote temperate, worthwhile forms of recreation that would restore rather than destroy labour power.[25]

Historical distance is an excellent aid in identifying social structural patterns. Looking back from the twentieth century, the attempts of the nineteenth-century 'powers that be' to shape popular culture are apparent to all. Then as now, power to control other people's leisure was based on broader economic, political and ideological structures. Leisure has never escaped from patterns of stratification in the surrounding society. This is not in dispute. But to *what extent* has mass leisure been controlled from above?

A parallel school of thought maintains that during the nineteenth-century a work ethic was successfully imposed on the entire population with a legacy that, even today, leaves us embarrassed by leisure, and makes the workless, the unemployed and retired, feel useless.[26] To what extent is this true? Did the people really take their masters' moral teaching so thoroughly to heart? Nineteenth-century writers idealised work. This was true not only of industrial capitalism's apologists. Radicals such as Marx, Ruskin and Morris postulated a 'golden age' when work was fulfilling, and envisaged its return. But in popular culture, ever since the Industrial Revolution, there is impressive evidence that 'instrumental' attitudes towards work have always been prevalent.[27] The employee who looks primarily to his pay packet for rewards is not a product of twentieth-century affluence. Most factory employees have never regarded work as a sacrament. The industrial working class has always harboured some healthy scepticism, and often outright opposition to middle-class values, nowhere more evident than during leisure.

Nineteenth-century employers encouraged holidaymaking with a view to promoting respectable life-styles, but this moral entrepreneurship did not reign uncontested. Before the end of the century working men's clubs and commercial enterprises were organising holidays, and it was their efforts that stamped the character of Blackpool and other favourite resorts. The early soccer enthusiasts from public schools, and the churchmen who took the sport to the masses, were not seeking to promote the type of spectator sport into which the game developed. To a considerable extent the working class accepted new forms of recreation only on its own terms. Leisure has never been controlled to the extent that people's working lives and education have been imposed from above. During leisure people have always been able to decline 'approved' recreations, to do their own things, organise their own pastimes, and even appropriate for their own purposes facilities provided with other ends in view. Some nineteenth-century efforts to influence working-class leisure made very little impact. No amount of exhortation has ever persuaded the majority of factory workers to become church-goers, or to attend evening classes, while 'drinking' has remained a tremendously popular recreation. By the beginning of the twentieth century the middle classes were retreating to their new suburbs having abandoned hopes of civilising the working-class citizenry.[28]

Popular recreation has certainly been influenced by the efforts of churchmen, local authorities, other moral crusaders and commercial entrepreneurs, but in turn the aims and practices of the powerful have been modified by the people's reactions. This is the leisure dialectic. Which side has gained the upper hand? Throughout the twentieth century's growth of the leisure industries the dialectic has continued to unfold. From above there have been repeated attempts to control or at least channel the public's leisure appetites. Nineteenth century do-gooders and moralisers have contemporary equivalents. They have been joined by new recreational professions, some intent on spreading the heritage, others keen to preserve standards and traditions in our arts and sports, and yet others who hope to assist members of the public to identify and express their own interests. Commercial organisations sponsor market research and advertise. They endeavour to predict and channel popular taste with a view to profit. The public sector also attempts to forecast and respond to trends. Meanwhile people continue to make their own uses of the facilities others offer, and have retained a capacity for creating their own styles of informal sociability and formal associations.

Which side has gained the advantage is one of leisure's currently controversial issues. Has our leisure become increasingly planned and controlled, often in insidious ways by advertisers and other hidden persuaders, thereby making the very concept of leisure with its connotations of freedom into an ideology which masks the reality of control and exploitation? Or is authentic popular culture ascendant? Is it the people's tastes that determine which voluntary, commercial and public enterprises thrive or sink? As yet sociology has no agreed answers. But by refusing to accept leisure at face value, the subject insists on raising the questions.

There is one further issue of major contemporary relevance to extract from this introduction to the development of leisure in Britain. If leisure is becoming a pervasive quality rather than a part of life, where does this leave the forms of organised recreation that have risen from foundations laid in the nineteenth century? Does any further growth of leisure require an equivalent strengthening of these industries? Or are our recently built sports and arts centres in danger of becoming museums, like Covent Garden, preserving recreations whose authentic roots lie in a former era? Could we be entering a period comparable to the creation of industrial society, during which our forms of play will again be recast, alongside the meaning of leisure? We shall return to these questions in Chapter 8. A sociologically informed historical introduction helps in framing the questions, but cannot deliver the answers.

Roberts, K. c 1981) *Leisure*, 2nd edn,
U.S.A, Longman.

4

CONTEMPORARY BRITAIN AT PLAY

Previous chapters have debated the character of leisure, and described its growth since the Industrial Revolution. Here the emphasis switches to how we use this increased leisure time and spending power. As explained in this book's opening pages, there is no data shortage on 'who does what'. We know that, today, television is far and away the public's major leisure activity in terms of time accounted for, while alcohol is the most important single object of recreational expenditure. We can describe the age, sex and occupational profiles of the minorities who visit the theatre, play tennis, visit stately homes and so on. But the moment we ask *why* television and alcohol are so popular, and query the special appeal of the theatre, camping and golf, and why most of us resist their potential benefits, the facts cease to speak for themselves. Like its predecessors, therefore, this chapter does not close its subject-matter. In answering some questions, it poses others, and explains how sociology is now beginning to rephrase leisure's *why* questions so that, given further research, more comprehensive answers will be forthcoming.

Twentieth-century developments

Simply describing *what* we do is complicated by the fact that leisure habits are anything but static. The leisure scene has changed continuously throughout the twentieth century. It remains fluid. But it would distort reality to stress change at the expense of underlying continuities. Manifest uses of leisure have been transformed without shattering the foundations built following the Industrial Revolution. New recreations have normally replaced pastimes that played similar roles in individuals' life-styles, and have been promoted by familiar types of leisure industries.

Between the two world wars, two major innovations hit the leisure scene; radio and the cinema. During the 1930s the 'wireless' became standard domestic equipment, and the trip to the 'pictures' became a favourite out-of-home recreation. On the surface the net result was a revolution in leisure habits, but in fact a great deal remained unchanged. Membership of clubs, participation in sport, spectator crowds at sports events and involvement in hobbies were undiminished. The main victims of the cinema and radio were the theatre and music-hall.

During the 1950s television captured Britain. Today over 90 per cent of households possess receivers, and television-viewing accounts for a quarter of all leisure time. Spectator sports have been injured. Radio and cinema audiences began a steep decline in the 1950s. Magazine sales, though not daily newspapers, suffered. But once again, 'participant recreation' emerged unscathed.

At the beginning of the 1960s car ownership was still a minority status in Britain, whereas by the end of the decade the majority of households were motorised, and another 'revolution' in leisure behaviour had occurred. One of the most visible consequences was to turn the countryside into a mass playground. The number of trips into the country has more than doubled since the mid-1960s. Motorised families have also transformed patterns of holidaymaking. Week-long stays in hotels have declined in popularity, and the tourist trades have been obliged to gear themselves to the demands of mobile holidaymakers. Camping holidays have been a main growth area. Increasingly prosperous, car-owning families, able to spend more than the traditional Wakes Weeks away from home, have invested in caravans and tents, and devise their own tours instead of buying pre-packaged deals. But once again, behind these changes there have been impressive continuities. Although the private motor car has widened leisure horizons, television audiences are undiminished. Indeed, since the 1960s time spent watching television has edged upwards, aided by longer broadcasting hours, plus the spread of colour receivers which prove better audience-holders than monochrome models.

Since the 1960s there has been no single leisure arrival as spectacular as the radio, cinema, television and private motor car. Countryside trips and active outdoor recreation have continued their growth in popularity. During the 1970s there was a marked rise in spending on (colour) televisions and audio equipment.[1] Sports participation has been another major growth area, the most rapid increases occurring in sports that previously interested very small minorities. Squash, golf, sailing and badminton are prime examples. These sports are frequently named in surveys where people are asked to suggest activities they would like to take up. On this basis, outdoor and table tennis, ice skating, show and air sports also emerge as forms of recreation whose appeal could multiply.[2] During the second half of the 1970s there was a very sharp rise in indoor sports participation, made possible by the sports centres that appeared throughout the land, mostly financed jointly by local authorities and the Sports Council. Between 1973 and 1977 participation in indoor sport rose by a massive 140 per cent. Sports that benefited from television coverage recorded particularly spectacular growth-rates: 293 per cent for billiards/snooker and 272 per cent for darts.[3] Once again, however, it is necessary to stress the underlying continuities. Spectacular growth rates are most easily achieved from low take-off points. Over 90 per cent of adults have not become darts, billiards or snooker players, and the popularity of participant sport has not reduced interest in other forms of out-of-home recreation. Visits to art galleries and museums have also risen, though less rapidly. Participant sport remains a minority interest, and the 'active' minority mostly practise sport for only small proportions of their total leisure time. Sport has simply been a principal recent beneficiary of leisure's continuing expansion.

'Like replacing like' appears to have been the general rule as the public has responded to new leisure opportunities. The cinema assumed the entertainment role of the theatre and music-hall. Radio and television have encouraged people to seek quiet relaxation at home instead of in public houses. Spectators now follow sport on television, less frequently at live fixtures.

Families travel for holidays in private motor cars rather than trains and coaches. But the holiday remains a recognisable institution. The patterns into which uses of leisure time are divided appear to have changed only marginally. Unfortunately, once we attempt to discuss 'underlying patterns' our efforts become speculative. We have precise statistics on who plays which sports and watches which television programmes, but as emphasised in the opening chapter, we know much less about the motivations and gratifications that might shape the underlying patterns.

Soccer's missing millions

An over-view helps to keep apparently revolutionary growth-rates in perspective. It also enables us to understand why specific pastimes have declined in popularity. Soccer's missing millions are a prime example. In 1948–49 Football League Clubs sold 41 million tickets. Today attendances run at less than 25 million per season and are still declining. Between 1973 and 1977 the proportion of adults attending soccer fixtures fell by 28 per cent.[4] Heated debates as to whether dull tactics or hooligans are driving fans away may be good for television, but have little to do with soccer's predicament. The root of this spectator sport's problem is simply that it was extraordinarily popular in the past. There has been an all-round decline in watching live sport, and the sport with the most to lose, namely soccer, has been particularly exposed.

During 1945–46 there were 36 million admissions to greyhound tracks whereas today there are less than 10 million. In 1952 there were 1500 professional boxers, over three times as many as today. These older pastimes have not been completely lost. They remain popular. Soccer is still Britain's leading spectator sport. The situation is simply that the public now has a wider range of alternatives, and the older leisure industries have been unable to retain their former market share of the nation's disposable time and money. The pub, the music-hall, the theatre, radio and older seaside resorts have all found their appeal waning. Radio has enjoyed a minor revival since the advent of the transistor, but it no longer plays the role in domestic life that the 'wireless' built in the 1930s. The cinema's decline is still underway. Like spectator sports, it has found it impossible to hold its own against competition from television and the wider opportunities brought within the reach of car-owning families. It is not the behaviour of spectators who have deserted specific sports that needs special explanation. It is exceptional sports like horse-racing that overcame a general trend and increased attendances by 20 per cent between 1973 and 1977 that pose the mind-testing questions.[5] Similarly it is pointless to search for characteristics of volley-ball and badminton that explain their recent growth. They have simply benefited from an all-round increase in sports participation. Once again, it is the exceptions that require special attention. Cycling has inevitably lost ground in a motorised society, though there was a modest revival in bicycle manufacturers' fortunes during the 1970s.

Television

Why is television so popular? Since the 1950s it has reigned supreme as Britain's staple form of recreation. Adults average 19 hours per week, approximately a quarter of all leisure time. Teenagers prefer out-of-home recreation, but younger children equal the national average. No other single leisure activity can rival television in terms of time accounted for, combined with the proportion of the population, well over 90 per cent, that shares the habit. There are other leisure activities that involve the majority of the public, but these account for only small proportions of individuals' leisure time. Examples include holidays away from home and trips to the countryside. Swimming and dancing are popular recreations, but few people swim or dance for anything near the 19 hours per week we average in front of our televisions. 'The box' has no serious rival. Yet it is rarely listed when people are asked to name their favourite activities.[6]

The answer to television's popularity is simply that it is misleading to treat viewing as a single leisure activity. Different people watch different programmes for a variety of different reasons. It may be satisfactory for audience research purposes, but does it help to explain people's leisure behaviour when we aggregate students watching Open University broadcasts with households where a live set is standard background noise, part of the lounge furniture? Television is a prime example of how little we sometimes learn from leisure research's apparently comprehensive data mountain. It illustrates the need to search behind 'activities' and break down 'official' categories to analyse behaviour in terms of the actors' motivations and gratifications.

Leisure drugs

Leisure texts that rivet attention on the arts, sport and countryside recreation distort their own subject-matter. Nowadays leisure is much more likely to mean watching television, while in terms of spending alcohol, gambling and tobacco top the league. 'Drink' alone accounts for around a quarter of all leisure spending, equivalent to three-quarters of our national education budget, and over four times our spending on all out-of-home entertainment.[7]

Outlay on tobacco runs at only half the level for alcohol, but makes substantial demands on the budgets of the 40 per cent of all adults who still use cigarettes. Imaginative marketing must take a large slice of the credit. Smoking is now as common among women as men. Sustained advertising campaigns have transformed the image of the female smoker. She is now a sociable creature rather than the uncaring mother of needy children. During the 1970s cigarette smoking declined among middle-class males. In certain occupations, including medicine, the decline was very marked. Cigar and pipe smoking have only partly compensated. Manual workers, however, have proved less responsive to government campaigns publicising tobacco's dangers to health.

As with tobacco, the industry's persuasive marketing must feature prominently in explaining alcohol's share of leisure spending. It has involved a remarkable reversal of a long-term historical trend. In medieval England drink accompanied all celebrations and holidays. Indeed, beer was the staple beverage of the people. Three hundred years ago alcohol accounted for one-fifth of the nation's calorie intake (today it is approximately one-twentieth). During the nineteenth century consumption declined, partly as a result of temperance campaigns, but mainly due to the introduction of pure water supplies and, after the 1850s, the popularity of tea. Throughout the first half of the twentieth century consumption continued its downward slide as licensing laws, taxation and the appearance of alternative recreations increased the nation's sobriety. But since the 1950s consumption per capita has doubled. For this the suppliers deserve much of the credit. Women have won some strange allies in the fight for liberation. They are now welcome in most public houses. Juke boxes and live bands have lured the teenagers. The pub's fortunes have revived. It has adapted to changing leisure-styles and remains a favourite resort when people 'go out'. Sixty-seven per cent of males visit a pub at least once a month.[8] Even more important in raising consumption, drinking at home, with meals out, and at most other places where people congregate for recreation has become not only acceptable, but expected Wine sales have rocketed.

Why do we allow ourselves to be persuaded to spend so much smoking ourselves to death and drinking our minds to oblivion? This is the reality of Britain at leisure more frequently than healthy outdoor pursuits. Many smokers are addicted, but few 'drinkers' are physically dependent on alcohol. So why do we spend so much, in 1980 an average of over £3 per capita per week, on drink? As with television, explaining drink's popularity requires that we disaggregate the activity. Different people use alcohol in different places for a variety of reasons. Most visitors to pubs name the human company, not the beer, as the main attraction.[9] Alcohol's appeal can only be explained once we realise that it has become a companion to so many other recreations, and that to describe alcohol as the object of expenditure is often misleading.

Gambling

The total staked by Britain's gamblers exceeds spending on alcohol, but as the greater part of the outlay is returned in winnings, the losses are relatively modest. The Home Office describes only 20 per cent of adults as regular gamblers,[10] but most of us have an occasional 'flutter' – on the Derby, the Grand National, gaming machines or charity raffles. Thirty-five per cent of all adults do the 'pools', 9 per cent bet on horses or dogs at least once a month, and 4 per cent play bingo regularly.[11] Betting has grown in popularity in recent years. Casinos and lotteries have been the main growth areas.[12]

Various explanations of gambling's popularity have been offered. Halliday and Fuller regard gambling as analogous to religious experience; a widespread and complex neurosis that combines phallic and anal tendencies.[13] Sociologists' explanations of 'compulsive' gambling emphasise situational factors.[14] 'Hard' gambling situations, as in casinos, which offer successive opportunities and quick reinforcing pay-outs can trap punters into chasing losses and attempting to recapture 'thrill'. But most gambling is not compulsive and appears best explained as an inexpensive entertainment. In betting shops individuals can play at 'keeping cool', exercising skill and judgement.[15] Bingo offers excitement and sociability. And in all gambling there is the outside chance of a *coup*, the big strike. For the working class this is as likely a route to wealth as occupational success. But the main point to be made once again is that different types of gambling are practised for a variety of reasons. There is no one explanation for the popularity of either television, our leisure drugs or betting. To explain their appeal we need to disaggregate the categories normally employed in surveys of leisure activity and spending, and reclassify people's pastimes in terms of their motivations and satisfactions, a task on which sociology has now embarked.

Beyond activities

Most leisure activities, a list that runs to many hundreds of items, involve only small minorities, though sometimes for impressive proportions of their enthusiasts' leisure time. Less than 2 per cent of adults are actively involved in 'track and field', but during the season the activists devote many hours each week to athletics.[16] Soccer, still Britain's leading spectator sport, often makes heavy demands upon fans' time and money, but is watched by less than 7 per cent of adults during a typical winter month.[17] Angling is our most popular participant sport (if walking, swimming and dancing are excluded), but less than 4 per cent of adults fish at least once a month in the peak season.[18]

The manner in which the population splinters into hundreds of small 'taste publics' is superficially perplexing. What is it about the minority of anglers that makes them devote a great deal of time and money to a sport that most of us succeed in living happily without? The problem with this question is that it takes 'official' categories too seriously. The headings beneath which leisure activities are conventionally grouped – sport, countryside recreation, hobbies, tourism, entertainment and so on, reflect common sense and the leisure industries' organisation, but are devoid of theoretical justification. Watching television and 'drinking' can mean very different things on different occasions and, conversely, ostensibly different activities may play very similar roles in individuals' life-styles. Groups of adolescent males can be found on football terraces, street corners and in public houses. Are these uses of leisure really as different as suggested when one is categorised as sport, another as social and the third as drinking?

Specifically sociological leisure research is still in its infancy, but it has already demonstrated that leisure activities have meanings for their actors; socially constructed meanings which define the potential satisfactions, and which often diverge from 'official' ideas about what the recreations in question offer. The wilderness, golf, discos and soccer are overlaid by 'mythologies and mystiques' which become part of the attraction, or repulsion.[19] Once a leisure activity such as holidaymaking at the seaside is considered 'common', it loses its appeal to those seeking exclusiveness. School-sponsored recreation is unlikely to interest individuals who wish to state their non-conformity. Detailed knowledge of the activities themselves is of only limited assistance in understanding the appeal of Kung Fu, skateboarding, disco and pool. It is the meanings imposed on these activities by the participants that are crucial, and these meanings often prove related to identities based on age, gender and social class divisions.[20] Participants are rarely solitary individuals. Specific uses of leisure tend to appeal to definite sections of the public who pursue their interests collectively. Leisure activities are used to nurture relationships and consolidate identities with roots in other spheres. The effects of this nurturing and consolidating are then liable to influence the behaviour of those concerned at other times and places. Teds, mods, rockers and punks become 'real people' with whom parents, teachers, the police and employers have to contend. These aspects of leisure never surface in orthodox recreation research. Sociology is currently placing them on the agenda.

Soccer hooliganism offers one example of what sociology can deliver. The 'hooligan' label itself is an interpretation, a meaning, assigned to a type of leisure behaviour. This meaning is supported by police and soccer officials, has been popularised through the media, and assimilated wholesale in officially sponsored research. The label assumes that perpetrators are a deviant, psychologically disturbed minority. Sociologists who have suggested otherwise have seen their arguments brushed aside by the powers that be. But to explain the behaviour of young fans on football terraces, probably the most important point to grasp is that their conduct is essentially social. It is governed by social norms in ways that make the hooligan label, with its implications of unrestrained anti-social conduct, entirely inappropriate. Officials who enjoy administering a national sport, and television presenters seeking clean spectacles for armchair viewers, display a remarkable capacity for overlooking how violence has always played a role in certain sports, including football. The distinctive pleasures derive from the group identities that team games confer, and enjoyment increases the more intense solidarity becomes. All football fans know full well that violence, on and off the field, adds to the excitement.[21] Mock fights that occasionally trigger real violence are not recent phenomena; they have always been part of traditional football.[22] Spectators are not desecrating their game's traditions when they defend *their* territory and invade pitches to take possession of *their* turf, and emphasise *their* domination of the opposition.[23] Football terraces are not anarchic. Fans' behaviour is governed by detailed rules and roles. Investigators willing to spare the time have distinguished 'nutters', 'aggro-leaders', chant leaders and novices.[24] Aggro itself is highly ritualised. Actual physical violence tends to occur only when internal controls fail, sometimes having been undermined by the imposition of external, police control.

Adolescent males who attend football matches are not seeking passive entertainment. If they were, *World of Sport* and *Grandstand* would meet their needs. They follow their teams in groups because they enjoy playing the supporter roles. Even when matches are boring, the fans can enjoy the atmosphere, and relive their pleasures through intervening weeks with tales of blood and glory. Soccer grounds have become theatres where young people, free from parental control, can act out teenage styles that bestow desired identities. When the media deplore and thereby publicise the roles, their clarity and appeal often increase.[25]

Soccer hooliganism has attracted sociological attention because it has become such a well-publicised issue. It may be unrepresentative of leisure behaviour. But this one example, however untypical, is sufficient to underline how little it tells us to enumerate people's activities under official definitions. To describe teenage fans as 'watching soccer' or as 'hooligans' conceals more than is revealed. Sociology is now beginning to probe behind the accounts of reality presented by the leisure industries, other authorities and in mainstream recreation research, and the following chapters on the relationships between leisure and work, and the family, draw upon the insights that sociological perspectives can offer.

Orthodox recreation research's findings are less 'solid' than they appear when presented in columns of statistics. The facts and figures suggest precision, but the impression is spurious. The data tell us that we average 19 hours a week watching television, and that 7 per cent of us watch professional soccer. These statistics are not lies, but they are less than the whole truth. They tell us nothing about the spare time that is spent doing nothing in particular. This category is not listed in the standard research instruments. They tell us nothing about the importance of soccer to the 7 per cent who attend (at least once a month during the season), nor about whether the reported viewers actually watch and/or remember the programmes they claim to witness.

Data on leisure spending have an equally fraudulent character. The total volume can be raised or lowered depending on what is included and excluded. What proportion of outlay on clothing, cars, housing, do-it-yourself, books, electricity, postage and telephones should count as leisure spending? It can be argued that once income exceeds the subsistence level, all expenditure contains a discretionary, leisure component. Similar problems occur in estimating governments' spending on leisure. How much of the total spent on education and libraries should we include? And what proportion of corporation expense spending on entertainment and meals out should count as leisure? Motoring would feature prominently as an object of leisure spending if economists were able to separate leisure from other motoring costs. Sex should probably feature as a major leisure activity. It is quick and cheap, and therefore neglected by researchers, but extremely popular.

If leisure was a *fully* compartmentalised sphere of life, these problems would not arise. Industrialism demarcated work, but it never wholly disentangled leisure from family and community life. If the bulk of discretionary spending is not on recreation, should we conclude that it falls outside the scope of leisure research? Or is this evidence of leisure penetrating other areas? Searching behind activities to investigate the socially constructed meanings associated with different uses of time and money, and relating these to individuals' identities and related motivations, can overcome these 'boundary' problems. It can also expose patterns that have survived 'surface' changes in recreational habits, and as we shall see, it can explain why patterns vary between different sections of the public.

Sources of variation

The preceeding sections have argued for more penetrating analyses of leisure behaviour. There is an equivalent need for sociological imagination to explore *sources* of variation in leisure activity. Simply dividing the population by age, sex, place of residence and socio-economic status is not practising sociology. These exercises are preludes to, rather than, sociological analysis proper. In many spheres, merely dividing the public into demographic boxes has proved highly productive. Socio-economic strata differ sufficiently in educational attainment and political partisanship to suggest worthwhile hypotheses explaining success at school and party loyalties. But in leisure research these standard exercises have been less fruitful. Many of the conventional demographic breakdowns simply fail to 'work', which is another reason why little progress has yet been made towards explaining as opposed to simply describing the public's uses of leisure.

Common sense might suggest the importance of geographical proximity; that people's leisure habits will depend upon which facilities are within easy reach of their homes. In some cases geography definitely makes a difference. People who live nearby, visit the coast more frequently than others. But the distances they need to travel are unrelated to the likelihood of individuals using swimming pools.[26] Sports, leisure and community centres, theatres and cinemas need to be extremely local, within walking distance of people's homes, before 'nearness' boosts levels of participation. Beyond walking range, within a fairly wide radius that can be conveniently travelled by car for an evening or day out, distance to be travelled has no clear effects. This does not mean that the siting of recreational facilities is irrelevant. City-centre locations and sites along main transport routes not only make for ease of access but create public awareness of the facilities. The point is that individuals who live close by will not necessarily be overrepresented among the customers. Inner-city residents are not notably frequent visitors to nearby concert halls and art galleries.

Common sense may also propose hours of work as a major influence on leisure activity; that those who work the longer hours will have the least opportunity to play. In fact only exceptionally long hours, over 51 per week, appear to have an overall depressing effect on levels of recreational participation.[27] The evidence suggests that, beneath this level, shortening hours of work does not enlarge leisure opportunities but surrounds individuals with surplus time. The people who name time as a major constraint on leisure are those who work long hours and enjoy large incomes. The car-less and economically inactive list money as their main constraint, while young housewives name domestic ties.[28] The popularity of overtime is not the product of a lingering work ethic, or of the public attaching little value to leisure. The fact of the situation is that, for many people, higher income is the best recipe for widening leisure opportunities.

Hours of work are not completely irrelevant. In the USA and Britain, as working time has declined the hours gained have been used for leisure.[29] Shortening the work-week does increase leisure activity when income, occupational and life-cycle status are controlled.[30] But in real life as opposed to computer analyses, all other things do not remain equal as working time varies. Long hours are normally rewarded with above-average incomes. Short work-weeks are most common among women and the semi-retired, and the implications of these statuses override the consequences that, in isolation, would follow from their time-privileged positions. Reducing hours of work does not boost everyone's leisure opportunities; for many people there are much better ways of achieving this objective.

The effects of shift systems are similar. Unusual working hours may isolate individuals from the normal rhythm of life. Some of those affected fiercely resent being unable to fraternise with mates in pubs, attend soccer fixtures and watch popular television programmes. Shift systems are not popular, especially among gregarious young people, though a minority welcome the opportunity to pursue private hobbies and enjoy their children's company during the daytime.[31] Most people will opt for 'normal' day work, given the choice, but shift systems are now common. Approximately a quarter of the labour force is involved, and many families have learnt to accommodate their preferred life-styles to the time available. The effects of unusual hours of work on leisure habits are neither as powerful nor as consistent as may have been suspected.

Domestic roles and social class positions are more powerful predictors of recreational behaviour than where people live and the amounts of free time at their disposal. Age and gender are associated with marked differences in uses of leisure. Young people are exceptionally active in most out-of-home recreations. With marriage and parenthood participation sags, continues to do so throughout the life-cycle, and reaches its lowest ebb among the retired. Women are less active than men in out-of-home recreation, especially sport. Age and gender are useful 'predictors', but alone and unaided they 'explain' very little. There are wide variations in uses of leisure among both men and women, and within all age groups. Simply dividing the population by age and gender does not even suggest explanations of leisure patterns. It is merely a starting point – leading to the sociological enquiries and analyses that are reviewed in Chapter 6.

A cluster of variables conventionally grouped under the 'social class' heading – education, occupation, income and car ownership – is positively related to participation in most leisure activities. The richest 25 per cent of all households account for 46 per cent of leisure spending.[32] Car ownership is a major threshold. Surveys at country sites normally find that over 90 per cent of the visitors are car-borne.[33] Eighty per cent of holidaymakers in south-west England now travel by motor car.[34] Some types of recreation are less class-related than others. The appeal of certain sports, including angling, is classless. Others such as soccer have a predominantly working-class appeal. Informal countryside recreation (walking, sitting and driving around) is less class-related than more formal activities such as visiting stately homes and participating in country sports.[35] But across the entire spectrum of leisure activities there is a definite and positive relationship between levels of participation and social class. Chapter 5 will explore the nature of this relationship in detail, but before proceeding it is necessary to emphasise what social class fails to explain.

There are no clear divisions in *patterns* of leisure activity between socio-economic strata. The higher strata 'do more', but today there are no points in the social hierarchy where life-styles divide. It has become difficult to name examples of specifically middle- and working-class leisure habits. Activities that are popular within the white-collar strata also tend to be popular among manual workers. The 'quality' press, symphony concerts and the theatre draw their audiences overwhelmingly from the middle class. Attempts to export 'high culture' to the working class have been notoriously unsuccessful.[36] But even within the middle classes, most people read popular papers, and attend neither the theatre nor concerts. One of the major trends in leisure during the twentieth century, a silent social revolution, has been towards blurring class differences.

The leisure democracy

In Victorian England leisure habits were sharply class-divided. Professional men and their families took no part in the street culture of working-class areas. Middle-class recreation was relatively formal and home-centred.[37] Needless to say, there was always some overlap. Drink was and remains popular throughout society. It is not only the resort of the uncouth working class. Spending on alcohol rises with income.[38] But until the Second World War there were very marked social class differences in leisure habits. An individual's dress and leisure tastes were reliable guides to his class position. The northern working class bore the brunt of the hard times during the 1930s, while the middle classes, based mainly in the south, prospered and cultivated new recreations including flying and motoring. During this period, however, the radio was cutting through class barriers, as was the cinema, and television has continued the trend.

There are still some socially exclusive pastimes. Aspirant show jumpers need rich fathers. But the most popular leisure activities, such as watching television and taking holidays away from home, are now classless. And the distribution of leisure time no longer follows the same contours as other indices of socio-economic status. In 1975 the 'working class' did less work and enjoyed more leisure time than the middle class.[39] For manual workers there have been long-term historical trends towards shorter work-weeks and longer holidays, but for professional and managerial employees there have been no such consistent trends. On average today senior managers and the self-employed work longer than men on the shop floor, and prove as likely to work overtime and 'unsocial' hours when unpaid sessions are taken into account. Holiday entitlement is not as strongly related to social class as before the Second World War.[40] Paid vacations were still a middle-class perk in many firms throughout the inter-war years, and while the 'works' normally closed for only an annual week or fortnight, professional men, and teachers, took a month or longer. Subsequently, middle-class holiday entitlement has grown slowly if at all, while manual workers have substantially closed the gap. Leisure time has been democratised in so far as its distribution has ceased to follow income and occupational prestige. There is no longer any sense in which our economic and political élites can be labelled a 'leisure class'.

This trend towards a leisure democracy has been consolidated as class differences in leisure tastes and habits have diminished. The middle classes still 'do more', but usually more of the same things that occupy working-class leisure. Class divisions in styles of holidaymaking have collapsed. Hotels and camp sites, and continental resorts now cater for socially heterogeneous publics. The history of dancing illustrates this same process of democratisation. In the nineteenth century dancing styles reflected class divisions. New fashions were set in the 'high society' surrounding the royal court and filtered outwards, but rarely as far as the urban masses.[41] By the inter-war years, in contrast, all strata were practising the same 'modern' dances, though in different places ranging from society restaurants to local palais. Subsequently even these differences have evaporated. The main clefts now follow age rather than class divisions. Disco transcends class barriers, and it is the public in general rather than high society that dictates trends in fashion.

This is not to argue that we are all submerged by a common mass culture and use our leisure in identical ways. It is not even being suggested that social class makes absolutely no difference; we have noted that the middle classes 'do more'. The situation is simply that to identify and explain variations in leisure patterns we need to probe behind, to break down, the standard social indicators. In addition to asking what different leisure activities 'mean' to their participants, we need to explore the relevant 'meanings' of age, gender and socio-economic status to enquire exactly which characteristics of our work and domestic roles lead to different uses of leisure. And in our search for positive relationships we must not overlook the extent to which uses of leisure may be independent of other statuses. Indeed, the following chapters will argue that its autonomy is one of present-day leisure's most significant features.

5

WORK AND LEISURE

中心；有心性

Work centrality and its critics

Sociology has a long-standing interest, critics say an obsession, with the effects of individuals' occupations and related social class positions across life in general. Students can be forgiven when they define sociology as the study of social class. In all fields of research, ranging from the family and education to religion and politics, the effects of occupational status on attitudes and behaviour have been assiduously explored. Leisure has been whole-heartedly embraced in this line of attack. The 'long arm of the job' has been the most intensely researched problem in the entire sociology of leisure, and this research has borne fruit in so far as it has demonstrated that many uses of leisure are influenced by many aspects of individuals' occupations. Recently, however, some writers have queried whether our understanding of leisure may have suffered from this emphasis on the ramifications of work.

Since modern leisure is a product of industrialism, it is perhaps understandable that sociologists should have initially approached its analysis by studying the effects of people's jobs on their broader life-styles. Nineteenth-century advocates of 'worthwhile recreation' regarded work and leisure as complementary processes. So did capitalism's critics. Marx regarded the leisure offered to workers under capitalism as a means whereby labour could refresh, recuperate, rejuvenate and thereby reproduce itself, along with the relations of production. Later generations of researchers have used these 'theories' as points of departure. Some have explored how uses of leisure express values and interests nurtured in employment, while others have investigated how, for many members of the work-force, leisure offers opportunities to compensate for the frustrations and monotony of work in modern industry.

Sociological analyses of the work–leisure relationship go far beyond comparing the recreational habits of socio-economic strata. They dis-aggregate the Registrar-General's social classes and attempt to determine exactly which features of work have which consequences for leisure. They have shown that the effects of work are not confined to the differential impact of 'constraints' such as time and income. Leisure opportunities do vary with hours of work and earnings, but beyond these constraints, investigators have identified more positive spill-over consequences of work. They have discovered that their jobs can influence how individuals *choose* to spend whatever disposable time and income their occupations provide. The social relationships and career patterns that surround different jobs, and the extent to which work is intrinsically satisfying have been shown to affect the types of leisure activities that individuals seek to pursue, with whom the activities are likely to be undertaken, and how they are experienced. Sociologists' enquiries have shown that work not only determines 'how much', but also 'patterns' individuals' uses of leisure. Exploring the implications of work, therefore, helps to answer leisure's *why* questions. This is not in dispute. Controversy among sociologists arises only as to the strength of work's patterning consequences. How strong is the long arm of the job? Could sociology's preoccupation with work-effects have created a distorted portrait of leisure's contemporary role?

Many students of particular occupations have concluded that the types of work under scrutiny amount to more than means of earning a living, and act as foundations for entire ways of life. The title of a well-known study of miners, *Coal is our Life*,[1] illustrates this point. In his study of job specialisation among factory workers, Friedmann offers a series of arguments about how routine work encourages distinctive uses of leisure, all with the end result, though achieved in different ways, of making boring jobs tolerable.[2] He argues that some individuals use leisure to compensate by devoting spare time to hobbies and handicrafts which employ skills and talents denied outlet in employment. An alternative response to boring work, according to

Friedmann, is to carry the stoicism required to make a monotonous job tolerable into leisure, thereby lulling oneself into a state of indifference towards life and society in general. Another way of becoming reconciled to monotonous work that Friedmann discusses involves using leisure to escape into fantasy, emotional release and amusement that repress the individual's awareness of unhappiness. In his now classic study, *The Organisation Man*, Whyte argues that many aspects of domestic and community life in middle-class suburbs are explicable in terms of the modern business corporation's demands upon the life and personality of the salaried employee.[3] The analysis of white-collar work presented by Wright Mills incorporates the claim that the sensitivity to status generated in this type of employment leads to characteristic uses of leisure, such as emulating the life-styles and consumption patterns of the upper middle classes.[4]

Sociological research into leisure developed, initially, largely as an offshoot from the sociology of occupations. Hence the now weighty literature that abounds with testimony to work's pervasive influence, and when written persuasively, as in the books listed above, arguments emphasising the implications of work can sound convincing. But a moment's reflection is sufficient to rouse suspicion. According to Friedmann, whether leisure is spent being lifted to highs of excitement at soccer matches, or being dulled into apathy by television, or pursuing arts and crafts, routine work is likely to be the common determining factor. But if one type of work can lead to such diverse recreations, some sociologists are now inferring that rather than a powerful explanatory variable, occupation alone explains and predicts very little, and this chapter is basically sympathetic to these arguments. It recognises work's contribution, but makes the case for emancipating the study of leisure from preoccupation with work-effects. Occupational sociology's more flamboyant illustrations of the ways in which work governs leisure have been based on consistently unsatisfactory evidence. The suggestions are essentially insights, impressions and inferences rather than conclusions tested through systematic and comparative research. The manner in which the reproduction of these suggestions in textbooks has gradually accredited them with the status of facts may prove only that sociologists have become habitually receptive to claims that individuals' occupations are prime determinants of their entire life-styles. Maybe sociological studies of contemporary society need emanicipating from some of their discipline's traditions.

By now it will be apparent that while this book is a statement for a virile sociology of leisure, it is not endorsing every proposition about leisure that sociologists have uttered. Such blanket approval is prohibited by the sociology of leisure's domestic controversies. Previous chapters have argued that the study of leisure can benefit from a sociological perspective. This and subsequent chapters will be equally concerned to suggest that sociology in general can benefit from recognising the growth and contemporary role of leisure. Sociology can illuminate leisure, and from leisure sociologists have much to learn about the character of their present-day societies. The latter have changed since the era when many of sociology's still dominant concepts and theories were forged.

The historical fact that leisure was shaped by industrialism may appear to justify the assumption that the best way to understand how people use their free time will be in relation to their jobs. But what if the character of leisure has again been reshaped since the Industrial Revolution? The contemporary significance of any institution is not necessarily explained by its historical origin. Although initially a product of the economic order, we must at least entertain the possibility of leisure having established a different role. Everyone recognises the persistence of some work-effects. But some of us also insist on recognising the extent to which leisure has become insulated from work. As argued in the last chapter, leisure time and activities have been democratised. People in all types of occupations are now able to make choices about what to do in their leisure from a wide range of interests and activities. This is why preoccupation with work-effects can create an unbalanced view of the work–leisure relationship, and an emasculated caricature of leisure's contemporary role.

Some writers argue that for many people leisure has now become such a major part of life that their behaviour and attitudes towards work are governed by leisure interests and values. This is one part of an argument, further instalments of which are presented in later chapters, alleging that we are heading towards a 'society of leisure', and in my view this theory deserves as sceptical a reception as 'work centrality'. The present chapter argues not that leisure is all-important, but that, in relation to work, leisure today is neither subservient nor domineering.

Work as a constraint

Few uses of leisure completely escape the shadow of work experience. Practitioners in most occupations watch television for a great deal of their leisure time, but this statement means little more than saying that virtually everyone walks and talks. As argued in Chapter 4, different people watch different programmes for a variety of reasons. Beneath the mass façade it is possible to identify a number of 'taste publics', many related to occupational stratification. White-collar employees view slightly less frequently than manual workers, when they watch television they are the more likely to tune to the BBC, and watch current affairs and documentary programmes.[5] It is pointless to search for any single cause of all these class-related variations in uses of television. As already indicated, different aspects of work have a variety of implications for uses of leisure, and the overall social geography of televiewing is the outcome of a large number of interacting processes. Nevertheless, beneath all the overlapping and interacting causes and consequences it is possible to identify certain recurrent patterns, one of which we have already encountered: the middle classes 'do more'.

The figures in Table 1, taken from the 1973 General Household Survey, give the proportions of respondents who had taken part in different leisure activities during the four weeks prior to their interviews, and illustrate the positive relationship between involvement in most forms of recreation and social class. Attempts to identify clusters of leisure activities that 'hang together', and which are associated with different social groups, have been frustrated by the fact that the same types of people tend to be the more active in most types of recreation.[6] Needless to say, there are exceptions to the 'rule' that the middle classes 'do more'. Darts and soccer draw their followers mainly from the manual strata. In discussing uses of leisure the middle- and

TABLE 1 *Occupational status and recreational behaviour, percentages taking part during previous four weeks*

Recreational activities	Occupational strata			
	Professional and managerial	Other non-manual	Skilled manual	Other
Active outdoor	27	19	18	10
Active indoor	13	11	12	6
Watching sports	11	10	13	7
Outings	27	26	20	16
Cultural	22	23	15	12

Source: A. J. Veal, *Leisure and Recreation in England and Wales 1973*, Countryside Commission, Cheltenham, 1976.

working-class concepts are sometimes a misleading shorthand. The middle classes are not uniformly active and the manual strata consistently passive. Levels of participation in many types of recreation differ little between the routine non-manual and skilled working classes. In outdoor participant sport, the main breaks occur beneath the professional and managerial groups, and above the non-skilled manual strata. It is only in 'cultural' interests such as theatres and concerts that the white–blue-collar cleavage becomes at all prominent. But notwithstanding the intricacies, across leisure as a whole, and particularly when the extreme points in the hierarchy are compared, a definite and positive relationship between occupational status and levels of participation can be discerned. American investigators have discovered a positive relationship between occupational status and organisational memberships, church attendance, political activity, sports participation, amount of reading, gardening, listening to records, interest in classical music, ballet and informal social activities. Over time there has been a general rise in participation, but social class differences have persisted.[7] United Kingdom findings offer a broadly similar picture. And the main explanation is not that the uncouth working classes prefer to idle time away doing nothing in particular, or that they are unaware of the many interesting things they could do. The main reason why the middle classes do more is that they command the superior financial resources. Cultural factors are not completely irrelevant. In response to survey questions the middle classes express the greater interest in sport and countryside recreation.[8] But income is the more powerful predictor, and attitudes themselves are largely products of experience and opportunity.

The last chapter explained that the availability of leisure time no longer follows social class lines. In any case, we also noted that time-effects on levels of recreational activity are modest; particularly so when compared with the implications of income and car ownership. The constraints of working time are sometimes entirely overridden by the countervailing influence of income. Within the professional and managerial strata, the length of the work-week is *positively* related to levels of recreational activity. Middle-class strivers who log marathon work-weeks are usually well rewarded financially, and can therefore afford 'full lives' during the leisure time that remains. Among manual workers long hours of work are also rewarded with above-average pay, but the net effect is a slight reduction in levels of recreational activity, the extra income being absorbed by domestic projects.[9] Middle-class workaholics can reach the stratosphere of second-home-owning, two-car families, whereas shop-floor overtime cowboys are more likely to be struggling to meet mortgage repayments on their only homes, and worried about the cost of replacing their second-hand motors.

As they are not time-privileged, there is a sense in which the middle classes are unable to 'do more', and their high levels of participation recorded in surveys are partly deceptive. The prosperous middle classes tend to 'dabble': they can afford the equipment to do a little of a lot of things, while the manual strata concentrate upon a smaller range of favoured pastimes, and investigations such as the General Household Survey that employ 'minimal' measures of participation, recording individuals as active if they have participated at least once during a given period, exaggerate the extent to which the middle classes 'do more.[10] But the evidence from these surveys is not wholly misleading. The manual strata idle the greater quantities of time passively, doing nothing in particular, or watching television, and lack of income is the principal constraint that explains this behaviour. As the retired and unemployed will testify, non-working time may not be leisurely. Without cash to spend individuals can find themselves with surplus time rather than the ability to express their interests and choose to do whatever they wish.

The middle classes are no longer time-privileged, but they still enjoy the superior incomes. Low-income and car-less families are clustered within the working class. Income is the best single predictor of sports participation; hence the prominence of middle-class participants.[11] The most strenuous attempts to deliver sport to the urban working class have recorded only modest success. Even when sports facilities are sited in working class areas, as with the Sobelle Centre in Islington, the clientele is found to consist mainly of the middle classes from further afield.[12] Suspicions that the main barriers to working-class participation must be cultural rather than financial are roused by the fact that the middle classes make the greater use of free facilities such as the countryside. But while the facilities themselves may be free, or available at nominal cost, access and equipment can be very expensive. Families unable to afford private motor transport suffer a general disadvantage in access to all leisure facilities other than those sited in their immediate neighbourhoods. This is the main reason why lower-income groups are the least active in virtually all types of out-of-home recreation.[13] And income inequality is the main reason why, across leisure as a whole, the middle classes 'do more'.

Spill-over consequences

Above and beyond whatever constraints they impose and thereby limit leisure opportunities, jobs have 'spill-over' consequences and influence individuals' preferences – how they exercise whatever scope for choice is available. These spill-over effects have attracted a great deal of attention, largely because they are less self-evident, more insidious and therefore more exciting to discover than the relatively 'obvious' constraints associated with time and income.

Spill-over is an umbrella concept covering a number of different processes, none of which operate universally, and as previously mentioned, the main issue under debate is not whether the processes ever occur, but the extent of their influence and what switches them on. *Compensatory* leisure is a kind of spill-over where leisure is used to recuperate, to 'recharge the batteries', discharge tensions, release frustrated energies and inclinations, to recover and 're-create' the individual prior to a return to work. We have already encountered Friedmann's suggestion that individuals subjected to monotonous factory jobs may compensate by devoting their leisure to creative pastimes, and Clarke found some supporting evidence in his study of 599 American males.[14] Handicraft-type hobbies were prominent within the lower occupational strata, and rose to another peak in the highest occupational group, possibly in reaction to desk-bound office jobs. Gerstl's American study of professors, admen and dentists found that the latter two groups often explained their interest in sport in terms of releasing the tensions of the work-day.[15] It is not difficult to discover examples of compensatory leisure, but this type of spill-over is far from universal. The majority of the non-skilled workers in Clarke's investigation did not devote their leisure to handicrafts.

Extension is a second type of spill-over, referring to instances where individuals use non-working time to employ or develop knowledge and skills, or cultivate social relationships relevant to their occupations. Clarke's finding that the top occupational strata were the most likely to spend leisure reading and studying is explicable as extension, and likewise Gerstl's evidence of admen using golf and dentists using voluntary associations to lubricate business contacts. Some corporations expect their executives to display this commitment; to use their homes as extensions of the office when necessary. Hence the American practice of 'wife-vetting'. Tupperware is one of a number of firms that deliberately use their agents' social networks to market their products.[16] Like compensation, extension is a far from universal process. The majority of British managers appear unwilling to subject their domestic and social lives to their employing organisations.[17] They are more likely than their American counterparts to proclaim their determination to leave work at the office. Why do these cross-cultural differences arise? And why are there intra-occupational variations in individuals' willingness to devote leisure to work-related activities? No one has yet offered convincing accounts.

Explanations are available as to why the extension of work interests is more common in certain occupations than others. This kind of spill-over is most probable when individuals' jobs are socially esteemed, and when both the work itself and the social relationships that surround employment are *intrinsically satisfying*. Such jobs are liable to capture the worker's ego, sometimes producing a workaholic. Parker found evidence of this extension pattern among the youth employment officers and child care officers whom he investigated.[18] In contrast, when work is physically arduous or otherwise disagreeable, Parker argues that individuals will tend to draw a firm distinction between work and leisure, define leisure as the very opposite of work and use their free time to seek distinctly non-worklike experiences. Parker completes his typology with a midway neutrality pattern, said to characterise occupations such as banking where the work is neither enthralling nor disagreeable. He argues that such jobs encourage individuals to regard work and leisure as simply different, complementary parts of life, each yielding its own satisfactions. Parker is not arguing that individuals who find their jobs satisfying will use their leisure in entirely different ways compared with people whose work evokes negative feelings. His main argument is that the meaning of leisure, whatever activities it encompasses, will differ depending on the meaning of work. There is independent evidence, however, that the extension of work interests does lead to distinctive leisure activities. Champoux administered semantic differential tests to 178 employees in an American pharmaceutical firm, distinguished those whose definitions of work and leisure were similar and different, and found that the former cultivated the greater number of hobbies and recorded the higher levels of activity in voluntary associations.[19]

The likelihood of work extending into leisure depends upon whether individuals find their jobs satisfying and invest their 'selves' in their occupations, and also upon the *styles of sociability* that different types of work encourage. Certain conditions of work are particularly hospitable to the formation of 'occupational communities', distinguished by their strong inter-personal relationships and consciousness of kind. Such communities arise in occupations which thrust practitioners into regular contact and relations of dependence, as in coal-mines, and where individuals' jobs isolate them from people in other walks of life, as among trawlermen. Salaman has shown that, albeit for entirely different reasons, strong occupational communities have arisen among London architects and Cambridge railwaymen, and in each case social relationships formed at work together with occupational interests pervade practitioners' non-working lives.[20] When conditions of work are not conducive to the formation of occupational communities, as among the 'privatised' car assemblers and other 'affluent' Luton workers studied by Goldthorpe and his colleagues, work problems and colleagues tend to be left at the factory gates.[21]

As with other work-effects, occupational communities do not spread into leisure with common and universal consequences wherever they arise. Allan's 41 interviews in an East Anglian commuter village suggest that friendship can mean different things in different social strata.[22] He discovered that the middle classes cultivated the wider circles of friends; working-class socialising tended to be concentrated among kin. In addition, he noted that working-class friendships tended to remain situation-specific, producing 'mateyness' within given locations such as at work, and sometimes in pubs. Working-class sociability appeared to arise by 'structured chance', when individuals who happened to be engaged in the same activity also happened to find they liked each other, whereas middle-class friendships were the more likely to become decontextualised and flow freely from setting to setting. It was quite normal for the middle classes to entertain friends from work in their homes. In this sense middle-class friends were consciously 'chosen'. In contrast, although their social relationships were equally cordial, manual workers' mates were unlikely to be invited into each others' houses. Sociability arose 'by chance' in various milieux, but was rarely taken further. The manner in which occupational communities influence their members' uses of leisure, therefore, may vary depending upon the styles of social life to which the individuals concerned are independently committed as a result of customary practices in their homes and neighbourhoods.

The shape of the *career pattern* is a further work-based variable with implications for uses of leisure. In the USA Wilenski has observed that orderly careers, that is, predictable and progressive movements between related kinds of work, are associated with high levels of social participation as measured, for example, by membership of voluntary organisations.[23] Wilenski uses this evidence to illustrate how, by giving a person a definite status and identity within society, the orderly career can help integrate the individual within the wider social structure. In a study of British managers Lansbury has confirmed that 'patterns of work and leisure are strongly influenced by career orientation'.[24] All Lansbury's subjects were in jobs of similar status, but he was able to distinguish *functionaries* who saw their present jobs as stepping stones within their organisations, *careerists* who hoped to spiral upwards within their specialities by moving between organisations and *academics* who were distinguished by their interest in research. These different career orientations were associated not only with the things the managers did during their leisure, but also with their attitudes towards these activities. Academics allowed work interests to penetrate leisure, whereas functionaries made firm distinctions between these spheres of life. The functionaries' leisure tended to be home-centred, the careerists devoted more time to socialising such as through informal visiting, while the academics were the 'culture vultures' recording high levels of interest in concerts, art galleries and the cinema. The significance of Lansbury's enquiry lies not in producing *the* definitive findings on how work affects leisure, but as a reminder of the many features of work, the career pattern as well as the social class position, income, hours of employment, colleague relationships and intrinsic job satisfaction, that can be influential.

Compartmentalisation

Some writers add together the many ways in which work affects leisure to conclude that 'work experience is a central determinant of the amount and type of leisure demands an individual will make',[25] and emerge with a *work centrality theory*. Work is portrayed as the governing influence which structures individuals' life-styles. According to this view, when people are not actually working, they are either preparing, recovering or otherwise deeply influenced by its demands.[26]

As mentioned on commencing this survey of the work-lei-
sure relationship, other writers are now seeking to emancipate
the analysis of leisure from the study of work-effects. They
argue that leisure is sufficiently compartmentalised from work to
confer genuine choice, that the attention paid to spill-over processes has exaggerated their true impact and that adding
together the various work-effects overstates their net weight.
They point out that not everyone is a compensator or an exten-
der of work-related interests, and that even when these types of
spill-over occur they usually account for only a fraction of the
leisure of the people concerned. Individuals in routine jobs *may*
compensate with leisure interests that require skill and autonomy, but their work does not oblige individuals to react in this
way. People in jobs that are intrinsically satisfying *may* carry
work interests and social relationships into leisure, but they need
not do so. Their decisions will depend upon whether they
possess other interests, and accommodating families.

For some people work operates as a central interest that structures and gives meaning to life as a whole. But how typical are
these individuals? Studies of industrial workers suggest that
work operating as a central life interest is the exception rather
than the rule.[27] Kelly is one of the few sociologists to recognise
explicitly his discipline's limitations when handling leisure.[28]
Following his investigations in three American communities,
Kelly stresses the independence of leisure from *all* social predictors. He argues that there is real scope for choice during leisure,
and chastises investigators who define leisure in terms of freedom, then seek out determinants, and remain dissatisfied while
their explanations stand incomplete. Kelly discovered relationships between his subjects' jobs and their uses of leisure, but
stresses that these relationships were far from watertight. Some
leisure interests were explained, by the actors, in terms of contrasts with or relevance to their jobs. But Kelly's informants did
not regard their occupations as relevant to the majority of their
pastimes, and locales and companions were mostly unrelated to
work. In his British enquiry among 736 males, Bacon found his
respondents' reasons for participating in various activities bore
little relationship to their social class positions, and his measures

of work alienation failed to distinguish different uses of leisure.[29]

Nobody argues that work makes absolutely no difference. It illustrates how other social statuses 'pattern' uses of leisure time. The arguments concern only the strength of these patterns – the extent to which leisure can be explained in terms of work-effects, and compartmentalisation theorists object only to analyses that dwell on the positive relationships that can be discerned and ignore the evidence that does not fit. Dumazedier admits that there are differences, but insists we recognise that the contrasts between their uses of leisure are by no means as sharp as between the jobs of managers and unskilled workers.[30] Many leisure interests straddle occupational and social class lines. There are inter-class variations, but why not emphasise the fact that in all strata television is a major leisure interest, that alcohol accounts for a substantial proportion of leisure spending and that only a minority of adults, albeit varying in size (during 1973) from 10 to 27 per cent between the extremities in the social hierarchy, participate in outdoor sport during any typical four-week period? Most leisure interests overlap occupational boundaries. Equally to the point, there are wide variations in uses of leisure among individuals performing the same jobs.

Even constraints may be less rigid than the term suggests. The low incomes on which some families have to exist place certain life-styles beyond the bounds of possibility, but without determining exactly what these families must do within the limits their incomes and hours of work permit. Their low incomes dictate that some individuals must 'do less' than others without decreeing exactly 'what'. Rather than determining uses of leisure in definite directions, the compartmentalisation theory treats work-based interests and social relationships as resources upon which individuals may or may not choose to draw depending upon the particular life-styles they wish to develop. Kelly reminds us that one of the essential and definitive characteristics of leisure is that individuals have scope for choice irrespective of their occupations and other social roles, which is why leisure can be genuinely creative.[31] There is an opposing point of view, which we shall repeatedly encounter in the following chapters, that dismisses the everyday meaning of leisure as ideological and insists that the appearance of freedom is an illusion. Exponents of this position insist, among other things, that in reality uses of leisure are strongly patterned by other social roles, but my own reading of the evidence accords with Kelly's conclusion – that the patterns imposed by work are weak rather than powerful. In real life individuals are not restricted to selecting activities from the fixed checklists used in social surveys. Individuals, families and friends can innovate, experiment with new uses of leisure, devise new sports and games, and sometimes evolve novel lifestyles. Sociology has demonstrated the ease with which relationships can be discovered between individuals' behaviour in all spheres of life. Societies are systems of interrelated parts in which everything tends to be related to everything else in some way or another. This is why it is so easy for investigators to make interesting and suggestive discoveries. Studies that rivet attention upon relationships between uses of leisure and occupational roles are not 'wrong', but could nevertheless be responsible for creating a distorted view of the role leisure now plays in people's lives.

The influence of leisure upon work   Growth

The work centrality theory's critics claim that historical trends are progressively diminishing work's determining power. There is no statistical evidence to test whether, over time, correlations between work factors and uses of leisure have become weaker. Earlier generations of social scientists did not collect the evidence we would now like to have available to appraise recent theories. But some writers nevertheless insist that a reduction of work's influence must be the inevitable sequel to a number of interacting and on-going trends. It is argued that as the population has grown more affluent, an increasing proportion of the possible range of leisure activities will have been brought within the reach of ever-widening sections of the public. Similarly, as the volume of time free from work has expanded, it is argued that opportunities to develop autonomous leisure interests will have grown correspondingly. Attention is also drawn to the growth of the mass leisure industries and mass media which, it is claimed, spread similar tastes and opportunities throughout society.

It is argued that work is receding in importance not only in terms of the proportion of lifetime it accounts for, but also in our value system. Once upon a time, it is suggested, people's lives if not their minds were governed by a work ethic; their occupations fixed individuals' statuses in the community, and thereby their identities. Hence the powerful patterning consequences of their jobs. The everyday getting acquainted question, 'What do you do?' has ordinarily been taken to mean 'What work?' Engineers, doctors and glassmakers have not merely practised and derived livelihoods from these occupations. They *were*, maybe still *are* engineers, doctors and glassmakers. When stripped of their work roles, individuals have faced identity crises. Hence the fear of retirement and unemployment. Loss of his work role has denied a man more than income. It has stripped him of social status, sometimes of all sense of personal worth.

This remains true today – for some people. Why else are some redundant executives known to conceal their predicaments from neighbours, even their own families? But is it not the case that the growth of leisure is now supplying alternative arenas for acquiring status, identity formation and maintenance? Some sociologists claim that status divisions are replacing class stratification; that we are ceasing to place ourselves and each other according to how we work and earn our money, and that how we consume, the life-styles we develop in spending our incomes, are becoming increasingly important.[32]

Nels Anderson alleges that from being an unintended by-product created by the unanticipated productive power and prosperity that industrialism unleashed, leisure has now grown to become the central element in many people's lives.[33] He argues that the expansion of leisure, creating new opportunities for people to develop interests, combined with the meaningless nature of so many industrial occupations, is encouraging more and more people to focus their main aspirations upon leisure. Historically leisure may have been a creation of industrial work, but today, Anderson argues, it is leisure that imparts meaning to work for the bulk of the population. Do most people use most of their leisure to compensate or extend work experiences, or is it more common for leisure to impart meaning to otherwise meaningless jobs?

If questioning the centrality and determining power of work disturbs sociology's conventional wisdom, it could be the latter that is mistaken. Maybe one problem with sociology's wisdom is that so much of it is conventional. As previously hinted, leisure has lessons for sociology. The discipline was created during the nineteenth century as a series of attempts to understand the emergent 'industrial' society, and the concepts and theories that were fashioned by the subject's founding fathers have remained central to the discipline's debates. As a result, contemporary sociology is well equipped to relate the present to the past, to explain how our current economic, political and educational institutions, and leisure, have been shaped by the rise of industrialism. But the sociology of the nineteenth-century founding fathers was originally forward-thinking, concerned above all to chart the contours of an emergent age. Contemporary sociology has relatively little to say about probable and possible futures. To understand present-day trends, maybe the subject needs new concepts and theories. The study of leisure could be one source of the necessary inspiration.

Having asserted its independent ability to give meaning to life in general, some observers proceed to claim signs of leisure reshaping the organisation of work, with leisure values such as pleasing oneself and doing things for their own sake invading the work environment. Fred Best believes that America, with other advanced industrial countries in its wake, is on the verge of becoming an 'abundance society' in which people will work not primarily to satisfy their material needs but increasingly to enhance the quality of their lives.[34] Hence the predicted demise of authoritarian management and routine jobs as workers refuse 'wage slavery' on monotonous assembly lines, demand satisfying work and opportunities to 'participate'. Dumazedier envisages a time when industry will be obliged to adapt to leisure values. He foresees workers insisting upon pleasant working conditions, seeking recreational facilities among their fringe benefits and demanding that social relationships within their firms are agreeable and friendly. In other words, Dumazedier anticipates a grass-roots movement towards a leisurely atmosphere at work.[35]

The concrete examples of leisure reshaping work that exponents of this theory can currently present may appear trivial.

Within shipyards the lunch-hour card game is a source of job satisfaction and a basis for group formation.[36] Business executives who are also family men often seek jobs that will provide security and status in their communities, and, above all else, insist that their jobs are located close to 'desirable' residential areas.[37] Dumazedier quotes cases of French managers who decide where they are willing to work on the basis of where they want to live, the latter being largely dependent on the local leisure facilities. There are (increasing?) examples of managers and professional workers protesting their frustration with careers in large and complex bureaucracies, expressing interest in doing something really 'worth while', and asserting that work should be about more than earning money.[38] Some opt out, forsake the rat race in preference for three acres and a cow. As yet their numbers may be trivial. To date the changes wrought in most jobs by leisure values may be marginal at best. But the current straws in the wind could nevertheless signpost the historical tide.

There is at least one clear example of leisure reshaping work which amounts to more than wishful thinking. Fred Best envisages freedom to choose extending to work schedules and predicts 'hours of work' becoming a normal topic for conversation at hiring interviews, the presumption of a standard 40-, 35- or even 30-hour week having grown outdated. Flexitime, which allows individuals to vary their working hours around a stipulated core, is portrayed as the beginning of a deeper transformation. Why not allow computers to synchronise individuals' preferred schedules with organisational requirements? Best talks of flexibility extending to the scheduling of work throughout the life span, with the now standard 'linear' sequence of education–work–retirement becoming just one of many options.[39] These forecasts are based on more than a vivid imagination. There are already wide variations in the hours worked by individuals in the same occupations.[40] Flexitime is spreading. The forms in which time has been shed from working life since the nineteenth century – the extent to which the working day, week and year have been trimmed, reflect workers' preferences as to the forms in which they wish to arrange their leisure time. Rather than the structure of leisure being dictated by a 'logic of industrialism', it is increasingly the case that the shape of working life responds to the public's leisure interests.

Leisure centrality is a highly controversial theory. Even exponents treat its propositions and forecasts tentatively. Few sociologists associate themselves with flamboyant predictions of work being wholly subordinated to leisure values in the foreseeable future. But even if our occupations are not becoming residual pastimes, there are grounds for stressing the extent to which the meaning of leisure and its uses have been freed from work determination. Today the most realistic approach to the work–leisure couplet is surely to presume that we are exploring a reciprocal and interactive rather than one-sided relationship.

6

LEISURE AND THE FAMILY

The family as a leisure milieu

Leisure and family life are thoroughly interwoven. Individuals' roles in the family based on age and gender affect their wider uses of leisure. Equally important, the family itself is a major leisure milieu. Despite the growth of the leisure industries, home and family retain pride of place as the most popular leisure resorts. The family is the milieu in which most of us first learn to play, and two-thirds of all the leisure interests we ever develop are initially practised with other family members.[1] When they visit parks, cinemas and other leisure facilities, individuals are more likely to regard these activities as extensions of family life than playing roles scripted by leisure industries. It is largely because the family is such an important leisure environment that the roles individuals play within it have a powerful influence on their leisure pursuits.

In most homes it is impossible to draw clear boundaries between leisure and other activities. Industrialism separated work and leisure, but it never divorced the family from recreation. In our society marriage is a voluntary institution, and the very acts of creating a home and family life can be regarded as leisure activities. Are family responsibilities always chores? Attitudes no doubt differ from family to family, and between members of the same households. Preparing meals and taking children on picnics *may* be regarded as leisure activities. Many people probably feel that such pursuits are only *partly* leisure, which brings us back to the problem of defining the concept. Is leisure a separate part of life which influences and is influenced by, among other things, family relationships and duties? Or is leisure better regarded as an aspect, a quality of family living and life in general? Because the family and leisure are so closely interwoven, their examination serves as a splendid entrée to the 'processes' that shape leisure, and whereby domestic, occupational and other 'factors' produce their effects, and as the family's theoretical significance has been recognised, the work–leisure relationship, hitherto the central issue in the sociology of leisure, has yielded some ground to the study of leisure in its 'natural', immediate, usually family context.

Leisure has been credited with helping to bind the modern family.[2] Some academic writers have echoed the folk wisdom that a 'family that plays together stays together'. Holidays and countryside trips are normally family occasions. Hence talk of the 'family car' as a vehicle fostering joint recreation and family unity.[3] If these claims have any substance, does it follow that non-family recreations threaten marital harmony? The family is important, but enjoys no monopoly as a leisure setting. Certain leisure interests normally entice their followers away from hearth and home. Whether of the participant or spectator variety, sport is only exceptionally a family activity. Despite the Sports Council's promotion of 'Sport for the Family', less than a quarter of visitors to sports centres enter in families, though the inclusion of a swimming pool can be relied upon to boost family use.[4] If leisure is growing, the significance of any ability to unite or divide families will presumably mount, and this is an issue that researchers are now beginning to explore. Is shared recreation associated with family cohesion and, if so, as cause or effect?

The importance of the family as a leisure locale, together with the fact that certain recreations appear particularly conducive to family unity while others drive family members apart, hints that it may prove useful to categorise leisure activities according to the types of participating groups they attract. As previously argued, common-sense classifications of recreations – into sports, the arts, countryside and social activities, have not been spectacularly successful in explaining variations in leisure behaviour, since the same people, usually those in the higher socioeconomic strata, tend to be over-represented in all the categories. As noted in Chapter 5, attempts to generate typologies by discovering clusters of activities that 'go together', that coexist in the same people's life-styles, have been frustrated by the same people tending to do a lot of everything, while others remain generally inactive. Instead of asking *which individuals* do which things, would it be more helpful to categorise leisure activities according to the nature of the participating *groups*, and to ask which activities attract families, groups of male colleagues, female friends, heterosexual couples and so on? Ostensibly similar activities may offer entirely different leisure experiences depending on the groups that participate. The gratifications that individuals seek and achieve may depend on whether they visit the seaside in families, or in monosexual peer groups.[5] In any attempt to develop such a typology of leisure activities, the distinction between family and non-family recreation will be an obvious starting point. Before long, however, typology-builders will find it necessary to recognise that 'the family' can mean many different things.

Is it realistic in present-day Britain to talk about leisure and *the* family? The phrase conjures images of 'normal' households; nuclear families containing breadwinning husbands, wives and dependent children. It brings to mind the idea of progress through a normal life-cycle with marriage leading to parenthood, followed by post-parental phases. But in 1976 only 20 per cent of British households consisted of children and two parents of whom only one was a wage or salary earner. A further 20 per cent contained children and two working parents, and 8 per cent, nearly a half as many as conformed with the traditional pattern of a breadwinner supporting his wife and offspring, were lone-parent families. The divorce rate has been soaring. Current trends indicate that 20 per cent of first marriages formed during the early 1970s will end in divorce within 15 years. In 1976 31 per cent of all marriages involved at least one previously married partner, compared with 18 per cent in 1951. Rising divorce rates are no longer construed as indicating a collapse or decline of the family. The majority of divorcees remarry. They are not fleeing from family life but creating new types of family career in which conjugal partners circulate, alternatives to life-long monogamy. Rather than heading 'broken homes', many single parents prefer to regard themselves, and are increasingly accepted, as different, not deviant. Cohabiting unmarried couples and the 'new families' in which several nuclear units live communally are no longer breaking away from consensual norms that prescribe *one* correct pattern of family living. Permissiveness has not swept all opposition aside. Homosexuals are still fighting their way 'out of the closets'. Whether they should be allowed to rear children remains controversial. But we appear to have long passed the point where it was possible to discuss *the* British family.

Different styles of family life carry diverse implications for leisure that researchers are only just beginning to explore. The National Council for Single Parent Families surveyed its members and found that, 'Nearly every lone parent interviewed described how, on receiving our letter requesting their co-operation, (they) had found the concept of leisure for single parents rather amusing. They felt that the National Council's contribution to the debate could be summed up by the question, *What leisure?*'[6] Surveying the variety of families forces leisure researchers to return to basics yet again, to reconsider the nature of leisure, for the residual, spare-time concept appears to have little relevance in lone parents' lives. The National Council's enquiry found that their main leisure aspirations were for more income and adult company rather than specifically recreational opportunities. Are lone parents odd exceptions? Or does this evidence support the view that rather than a part of life to be filled with specifically leisure activities, leisure today is better conceived as a variable quality of life in general?

Confronting family diversity also forces researchers to reappraise their evaluations of certain leisure activities. Television has been labelled a time-filler, facilitating 'para-social involvement', a poor substitute for 'real' leisure activity.[7] This may be the case for many of the 19 hours per week that we average, but for lone parents, according to their National Council, 'the television is the focus of their leisure', and disparaging 'telly addicts' may fail to recognise the value of this entertainment for adults who are housebound. Television is very important to a larger number of married women who are tied to their homes by domestic responsibilities. Dismissing television as suitable only for the incurably passive betrays a failure to understand these predicaments. Improving the quality of television broadcasts could make a greater contribution to their quality of life than funding opportunities for out-of-home recreation.

Domestic age

Uses of leisure change alongside 'domestic age',[8] a concept that combines chronological age and family responsibilities. As noted in Chapter 4, age roles and their associated domestic obligations are among our most powerful predictors of leisure habits. The differences that emerge are sharper than when age groups are broken down by social class.

Adolescence is the exception to the family's prominence as a leisure milieu. This is not because the majority of the young are pioneering long-term alternatives. They withdraw physically and emotionally from the families in which they were reared, thereby permitting the social and psychological developments leading to marriage, parenthood and the creation of new nuclear units. During the transition, however, young people are more responsive to the tastes and interests of peers than families. It is to standards established by their own age group that young people look for guidance on issues such as how to dress, what to do at weekends and what music to enjoy. The peer group becomes not only a prime source of leisure interests, but also displaces the family as the normal milieu for leisure activity. Young people spend a much larger proportion of free time outside their homes than any other age group. It is not uncommon for adolescent boys to spend five or more evenings each week with their 'mates'.[9] For the young, leisure means 'going out', and going out means with friends, not parents.

Because they spend so much leisure time outside the home, young people are important customers for the industries that market amusement and other recreational services. Cinemas, dance halls and coffee bars depend heavily upon young people at leisure. The popularity of commercial entertainment among young people has been accentuated by the rapid growth of teenage spending power since the Second World War.[10] The incomes of young workers have risen more steeply than adult earnings, and as their family responsibilities are minimal, adolescents are able to devote their wealth to entertainment. Manufacturers of clothing, music and other leisure commodities are keen to capture the teenage market. Spending by single women aged 15–29 on clothing, cigarettes, sweets, toiletries, cosmetics, records and cassettes runs at one and a half times the level for their married contemporaries, and four times the level for those in education.[11] Young people at leisure are big business. Affluent teenagers have been able to develop their own tastes, fads and fashions; youth culture is the generic label. Instead of following trends set in fashionable adult society, the young have become the pace-setters.

With their leisure based outside the home, and equipped with the financial resources to indulge their tastes, young people nurture a wider range of interests and pastimes than any other age group. Leisure activities including the cinema, theatre, travelling abroad, parties, meals out, dancing, records, classical music and simply getting to know more people arouse more interest among adolescents than in any other section of the population.[12]

TABLE 2   *Leisure and age – percentages participating during previous four weeks*

Type of leisure activity	Age group						
	16–19	20–24	25–29	30–44	45–59	60–64	65 and over
Active outdoor	32	22	22	20	12	10	6
Active indoor	21	17	15	16	6	2	1
Watching	18	15	12	13	8	6	4
Outings	18	25	27	26	20	19	13
Cultural	41	33	25	19	4	9	6

Source: A. J. Veal, *Leisure and Recreation in England and Wales 1973*, Countryside Commission, Cheltenham, 1976.

As can be seen in Table 2, the young are the most active age group in virtually every form of recreation, but especially in sport and 'cultural' activities which include the traditional arts plus all other performances to live audiences, except sport. The reasons for this hyperactivity include young people possessing the necessary time and money plus the physical capacity to enjoy active recreation, and having no homes of their own. But there is an additional, probably even more fundamental reason. Sociological studies of how leisure activities change during the life-cycle have clarified some of the processes whereby social statuses are translated into patterns of leisure behaviour. Their age does not directly 'cause' individuals to attend pop concerts or participate in sport. The Rapoports' study of *Leisure and the Family Life-cycle* has searched behind 'palpable demand' to identify the interests and preoccupations that encourage particular uses of leisure.[13] For adolescents self-identity is a major preoccupation. Youth is a process of transition; it involves learning new roles during which individuals must discard their former child-like selves and learn not only to behave but also to feel like adults. The Rapoports recognise that any one leisure activity can express a multitude of interests, and that the same interest may find expression in alternative leisure activities. In their view, young people's preoccupation with questions of identity leads not so much to any fixed choices of leisure pursuits, but to a general inclination to experiment with different activities and social relationships. Hence the flux, variety and overall high rates of activity by young people in all types of recreation. Kelly has noted that age is an excellent predictor, better than any other single status, of *what* people do during leisure time, but argues that it is an even better predictor of the *gratifications* they will seek and the *motivations* underlying their activities,[14] and it is by probing these 'meanings' of age and leisure pursuits that sociology can clarify and explain *patterns* of leisure behaviour. Young people are keen to develop new tastes, willing to experiment, and a net result is that adolescent leisure is often extremely colourful, particularly when set against the more stable and conventional habits of adults. Older generations continue to express concern, sometimes alarm, at young people's lack of respect for convention. But the plain fact is that the mainly domestic pastimes of older age groups will have little appeal to the young who are not claimed by family responsibilities.

Marriage and parenthood herald dramatic changes in leisure habits. Peer groups and out-of-home interests are forsaken for television and other domestic comforts. Family responsibilities mean that the amounts of free time and money available to maintain outside interests diminish. Establishing a home becomes a central preoccupation, and with this change, variety and experiment are replaced by a consolidation of a more limited range of pastimes. For most people, marriage is the beginning of a gradual decline in leisure activity that continues throughout the remainder of the life-cycle. There are exceptional people, and exceptional leisure activities. Countryside outings, drives and picnics are most popular during the child-rearing phase.[15] These are family recreations, like television viewing, and are exceptions to the rule of people doing less as they age. In general, as individuals grow older, they become progressively more likely to spend evenings at home, often doing nothing in particular. After marriage individuals cease to have disposable income to sustain colourful, out-going life-styles. In addition, they appear to lose interest in many former pastimes. They retain and consolidate some interests, but lose the urge to experiment.

In the USA Estes and Wilenski have written of morale sagging during a 'life-cycle squeeze' as the arrival of children and pressures of establishing a home oblige individuals to relinquish former interests and social relationships.[16] These authors invite us to regard rising divorce rates amongst the young as a response to these pressures. They have an undoubtedly valid case – in certain instances. It is not difficult to find young husbands and wives who resent their loss of freedom.[17] But death is still the most common terminator of marriage. Other individuals appear to welcome escape from the pressures of adolescence.

As people move into middle age, as children become independent and domestic responsibilities lighten, time and money for leisure often become available on an unprecedented scale. During this phase of the life-cycle there are *opportunities* for rejuvenated life-styles and an expansion of leisure interests. In practice, however, there is little evidence of a middle-age renaissance. Some couples revive 'nights out' for meals, concerts and other forms of entertainment. Activists in religious and political organisations are often drawn from this age group. But the re-establishment of leisure interests outside the home is exceptional. During middle life the overall trend is for leisure interests and activities to become increasingly restricted. More, not less time is spent at home.

Maybe individuals are preparing for old age. The retired are a minority, but a growing minority, and now account for one-sixth of the entire population. They are a heterogeneous group.[18] There are huge age differences among the old and retired. Many retired persons still have parents living. The experience of ageing differs between men and women, and between social classes. The retired are more likely than any other group to be impoverished, but contain some of the wealthiest people in the land. Overall, however, the evidence from leisure unequivocally supports disengagement rather than re-engagement theories of ageing. The decline in leisure activity underway since adolescence continues. The old spend enormous amounts of time at home. They are more likely than workers to complain of 'time on their hands'.[19] Many are constrained by deteriorating health, lack of income and transport. But interests also subside. The retired express less desire for leisure activity than any other age group. Recreation surveys implicitly acknowledge the inactivity of the old when they restrict samples to the under-70s, or even the under-65s.

As at earlier points in the life-cycle there are exceptional individuals and leisure activities. Some leisure interests peak in popularity among older age groups – mainly passive forms of recreation such as reading and television viewing. For the retired, out-of-home recreation centres on clubs and churches. The only form of physical recreation where activity increases with age is gardening. For years a body of writers has urged us to treat retirement as offering opportunities for re-engagement – to drop some activities in preference for others that are more fulfilling,[20] but this still remains hopeful thinking rather than a statement of fact. According to Parker, '. . . anticipated leisure is at the crux of the myth of retirement'.[21] Examining leisure and the retired forces us to treat the claims of 'leisure centrality' seriously and critically. To what extent can leisure replace work, and the family also in many cases, as a satisfactory base for social and personal development?

Gender

There was a time when gender differences were neglected, not only in the study of leisure, but across sociology in general. Liz Stanley reports that 67 per cent of the 'people' articles in the three main British sociology journals between 1970 and 1974 dealt only with men.[22] In a set of leisure research abstracts that Stanley analysed, only 3 per cent examined gender differences. Any future reviewer of the literature since the late 1970s will have a different story to tell. A revived feminist movement has made women's studies a major growth industry. A wave of publications has arrived dealing with gender differences in general, and the fates of women in particular in industry, crime, literature, education – and leisure.

'Telling the story' from the woman's perspective has helped inspire the radical critique of mainstream leisure research which attacks the very concept of leisure as ideologically loaded, unfit to be assimilated wholesale into social science. Apart from other sins, it is claimed that leisure is a masculine concept. Feminist critics have gone further than complaining that, on average, women enjoy less leisure time than men and that their range of activities is restricted, to query whether women are allowed to experience the same kind of leisure that men enjoy, and that is celebrated in conventional texts.

Hobson's searching interviews with 10 young working-class wives led her to question whether they possessed any genuine leisure whatsoever.[23] Housework is structureless. How much is enough? When does a housewife's working day end? Some women actually regard their paid jobs as a release from work.[24] The feeling that leisure has to be earned leaves some housewives doubting whether they have any 'right' to leisure. Hobson's young wives could recall the phase between leaving school and 'settling down' when they were able to go out for enjoyment. For these women, settling down began with serious courtship, not marriage. Upon becoming committed to a man they abandoned their own leisure interests and friends. Courtship and subsequently conjugal relationship were allowed to exclude all others, sometimes resulting in extreme privatisation following marriage.

This depressing portrait of the housewife's predicament has not escaped challenge. Tomlinson's account of the reflections of seven women from an adult education discussion group suggests that some wives freely exchange the leisure of childhood for a different way of life in which leisure experiences are derived from domestic and community 'work'.[25] From his informants' reflections on their own life-styles, Tomlinson infers that while in some senses a constraint, family life itself can be a form of satisfying leisure. Some women undoubtedly define shopping and cooking as leisure pursuits, but more men than women express interest in the latter activity,[26] and it would be foolish to attribute to choice the fact that, on average, women devote twice as much time to domestic work as men, even when both partners work outside the home.[27] Women, like working men, react to their situations in diverse ways. Some may glory in the delights of domesticity, but increasing numbers appear to resent the status of captive wives.

Feminist critics dispute the evidence from time–budget surveys,[28] suggesting little difference, on average, in the volume of leisure time enjoyed by men and women. They draw attention to the double shift of paid employment followed by domestic work to which many women are now subject. Furthermore, they argue, irrespective of whether they hold non-domestic jobs, women's family responsibilities can extend over 24 hours. In addition, housewives often have little money for leisure spending. When both marital partners hold paid jobs, the man still tends to be defined as the 'breadwinner' who is therefore entitled to his pleasures.[29] If they spend money on themselves, some women experience pangs of conscience for raiding the housekeeping. Women are less active than men in most forms of out-of-home recreation. Church-going and bingo are among the principal exceptions.

The evidence from the General Household Survey, presented in Table 3 shows that female participation in sport lags well behind male levels, and women do not compensate through greater involvement in other types of leisure activity. Their involvement in 'outings' and 'cultural' pursuits equals but does not surpass male levels, and some feminists claim that the appearance of equality in leisure apart from sport is illusory. It is argued that on their trips to the countryside and cinema, and while watching television, women often remain 'on duty' as wives and mothers, and sometimes participate not primarily for their own enjoyment but to service their husbands' and children's leisure.

TABLE 3   *Leisure and gender – percentages participating during previous four weeks*

Types of leisure activity	Males	Females
Active outdoor	24	11
Active indoor	14	6
Watching	15	5
Outings	21	21
Cultural	18	18

Source: A. J. Veal, *Leisure and Recreation in England and Wales 1973*,
Countryside Commission, Cheltenham, 1976.

Another explanation for women's lower rates of recreational activity is that they are less likely than men to have access to private motor transport. Men tend to exercise first claim on 'family' cars. And rather than bringing liberation, even a second car can further enslave the woman by making her responsible for ferrying children, relatives and neighbours. Women's leisure opportunities are further restricted by the fact that in some communities it is still considered almost improper for women to go out for leisure except in a family group or to visit relatives. There are many women who never 'go out' for leisure on their own or with their own friends. In addition, some never go out with their husbands.[30] Pleasures have been grasped vicariously, by servicing the play of husbands and children. For some women, this *is* leisure. Feminists argue that men enjoy leisure in non-working time only because they are cared for by wives, who are thereby denied equivalent opportunities.

The home and school have conspired to prepare boys and girls for different leisure futures. Boys are the more likely to be encouraged to develop out-of-home interests, in sport and camping for example.[31] During adolescence the leisure pursuits of girls are supervised and controlled by parents to a much greater extent than the lives of boys.[32] Even when women enjoy financial independence and are released from domestic obligations, these 'cultural' barriers continue to restrict their leisure horizons. Adolescent girls often devote immense free time and disposable income to constructing feminine identities. Middle-aged women whose children have grown to independence may find themselves with more spare time and money than ever before.

A third of these 45–60-year-old women in the post-parental phase do not work outside their homes. When young, the women concerned were rarely educated beyond the statutory minimum, and few received any vocational training.[33] Are they any better prepared to extend their leisure interests? In this age group it is men, not their apparently time-privileged wives, who maintain the greater number of friends and organisational memberships.[34] Women become more 'deeply' involved in a smaller number of social relationships, a style of sociability initially learnt during adolescence. When not constrained by time and money, women often remain inhibited by feminine norms which prevent them succeeding, often even trying to articulate and act upon their interests.[35]

Traditional sex stereotypes are dissolving, or so the literature says. It has been argued that the demise of the traditional family with its segregated sex roles, in which the only leisure opportunities available to women were among kin and neighbours, and its replacement by non-traditional units incorporating joint conjugal roles, will make leisure available to women on the same terms as their husbands.[36] In practice, however, there seems to be little merging of the roles of husbands and wives even within non-traditional families. The style of partnership that has become common is one in which spouses act as 'colleagues', sometimes companions, supporting each other rather than genuinely sharing their different roles.[37] American researchers claim that sex differences in leisure behaviour are slowly narrowing.[38] In Britain women are now accepted as customers in public houses, the Sex Discrimination Act having overcome the remnants of resistance. It is no longer safe to assume that unescorted females are 'on the game'. Yet even the most recent surveys indicate that we are still a long way from full sex equality and genuine symmetrical families.

Must we conclude that women have less leisure than men, or no genuine leisure at all, or are women's leisure styles simply different? We are back with that recurrent question: what is leisure? If leisure is becoming a quality of life in general, is it an implication that men's life-styles will become more like women's, and that feminists who seek to emulate male patterns are fighting the battles of a closing era?

Structurally determined or free?

Like practitioners in given occupations, women are a heterogeneous group as far as uses of leisure are concerned. Among
women, social class differences in levels of recreational activity
are wider than among men.[39] For working-class women, socio-
economic status and gender interact to produce extremely depressed rates of participation in out-of-home recreation. When at
home, their leisure activities tend to be narrow, sometimes confined to watching television.[40] Age, sex and social class do not
exercise their influence on leisure in splendid isolation but interact to foment a variety of life-styles, and in some observers'
eyes this diversity is equated with freedom, proof that leisure
lives up to its definition and allows individuals to pursue whatever their interests happen to be. The fact that women differ
among themselves in leisure habits, that some do participate in
sport and visit public houses, can be paraded as proof of what all
women could do, if only they wanted. In opposition, other commentators insist that this freedom is largely an illusion, and that
the leisure concept is ideological rather than a proper tool for
social science. The essence of this critique is that beneath leisure's diverse surface appearances we can detect very definite
patterns, some imposed by economic constraints, others derived
from the division of labour by gender, and it is argued that ana-
lysing their 'leisure' activities only obscures the deprivations that
women and other oppressed groups endure.

We first encountered this theory of leisure and its industries
as instruments of social control in Chapter 3. It reappeared in
Chapter 5 when considering the influence of work upon leisure.
A final verdict can be reserved until the concluding chapter, but
in the meantime we must assess whether gender differences offer
convincing support. No one denies that women's domestic roles
affect their leisure opportunities, any more than there is any dispute that low incomes circumscribe leisure possibilities. The
arguments surrounding occupational and family determinants of
leisure behaviour concern the strength of these restrictions. Are
they so powerful as to require the leisure concept to be treated
basically as an ideology that masks rather than explains reality?
My own view is that, as in the case of work, the patterning

effects of gender, and age, can be grossly overstated. The leisure opportunities of families on very low incomes are severely restricted. No doubt some women still spend lifetimes proverbially chained to kitchen sinks. But it is surely misleading to generalise from these cases.

Sociology's mission is to establish relationships between different aspects of social life, relationships of which actors may be totally unaware. People may believe they use leisure solely to 'do their own things', but sociology will draw attention to how their opportunities, even their preferences, are shaped by occupations, gender and domestic roles. The danger is that sociology will create the appearance of explaining everything. Such imperialism is unnecessary, and in the study of leisure it distorts the subject. Drawing attention to the fact that societies are systems of interrelated parts does not require insisting that all the relationships are rigid. Age and gender roles are among our best social predictors of leisure behaviour, but their predictive power falls well short of perfection. There is immense variation in uses of leisure among men, among women, among the young and among the retired. Relationships between leisure habits and other social roles are loose, not watertight. Most workers, most men and most women possess some scope for choice, and as they have acquired more leisure time and disposable income, this scope must have widened. There are still inequalities in the distribution of disposable time and income. But can there be any doubt that men and women in general, whatever their ages, whatever their occupations, have benefited from the growth of leisure? One conclusion that sociologists should not be afraid to draw is that their discipline cannot explain every detail of every person's leisure, and this is not just because our evidence is incomplete, the measurements inexact or our methods of manipulating data inadequate. Having weighed the evidence, some sociologists, myself included, conclude that leisure does fulfil its promise and confer freedom from social structural constraints.

John Kelly argues that while certainly influenced by other social statuses, uses of leisure are more responsive to 'situational' factors.[41] Whom we happen to be with on given occasions, our geographical locations and spur-of-the moment preferences can influence our conduct. Rather than irresistibly pointing individuals towards definite activities, Kelly argues that our positions in society carry implications for leisure mainly through the interests and motivations they encourage, which can normally be expressed through a range of possible leisure activities. While influenced by the social structure, Kelly insists that the public at leisure retains significant scope for manoeuvre. In his study of an American community, Kelly asked his informants about the reasons that led to the uses of leisure they reported. He was able to categorise activities, firstly, according to whether or not individuals were aware of external influences and constraints, and secondly, according to whether they were attracted by the leisure activities themselves or the other people who were involved. Combining these distinctions enabled Kelly to construct the typology in Table 4. Firstly there is *unconditional leisure*, activities pursued purely 'for their own sake'. Sport normally fell into this category. Secondly there are uses of leisure where individuals feel constrained, but not by social obligations. Kelly subdivides this category into two types of leisure: *compensatory activities* which are valued for their contrast with something else, usually work, and *recuperative activities* which individuals value as an opportunity to refresh or restore themselves, once again often following work. Watching television, reading and visits to the theatre often fall into this category. Thirdly there is *relational leisure* where the activity is freely chosen with the intention of enjoying or developing social relationships, such as during the

TABLE 4

Meaning of the activity to the individual	Perceived external influence/awareness of constraints	
	Low	High
Intrinsic	1. Unconditioned leisure — 31%	2a. Compensatory leisure — 5% 2b. Recuperative leisure — 25%
Social	3. Relational leisure — 22%	4. Role-determined leisure — 15%

Adapted from: J. R. Kelly, 'Situational and social factors in leisure decisions', *Pacific Sociological Review*, **21**, 1978, pp 317–30.

family outing to the coast or the round of golf with a colleague.
Fourthly Kelly's typology distinguishes *role-determined leisure*
where individuals feel they have to do certain things, maybe
tend the garden, as a result of social obligations.

Kelly calculated the percentages of his respondents' uses of
leisure that fell into each of these categories. Note that only 15
per cent of all activities were role-determined. The 'pull' across
the typology is 'north-west', that is, in the direction of activities
freely chosen for the intrinsic satisfaction. There is no need to
presume that Kelly's findings would be exactly replicated if his
study was repeated in some other community. Leisure activities
were placed into categories according to informants' accounts of
their motives, and it is fair comment to object that individuals
may not be aware of all the social forces that shape their conduct. But are individuals likely to be totally deceived? Does anyone imagine that all four of Kelly's categories would not be
populated wherever a similar enquiry was conducted? Kelly
argues that only a *pluralist* theory of society can accommodate
the reality of leisure. He opposes *holistic* theories that conceive
leisure as wholly determined by a totally integrated pattern of
life, and *dualistic* theories which treat leisure as occupying completely separate, autonomous life space. Kelly's pluralist, midway position insists that leisure is not unrelated, but neither is it
always secondary to the rest of life, that leisure behaviour is role-
related and not totally unpredictable, but simultaneously free in
the sense of offering genuine scope for choice. A pluralist theory
allows leisure to assume multiple forms and meanings without
generating conflict. According to Kelly, pluralism recognises
'the variety of opportunity and meaning that is necessary for
leisure to retain its defining element of freedom'. Kelly shows
that it is possible to analyse leisure sociologically without portraying its uses as rigidly determined by individuals' other social
statuses. The prerequisite is an appropriate, pluralist theory of
society.

Leisure and the quality of family life

If leisure is less than fully determined by other social roles, is it
possible that leisure could be a source of values and interests

that pervade other spheres? This is suggested by writers who foresee work becoming leisurely and scheduled according to leisure interests, and an even stronger case can be made for leisure's ability to penetrate family life. It is this kind of trend to which writers are endeavouring to draw attention when they argue that leisure today is better defined as a process, or quality of life in many domains, rather than a discrete part of life filled with purely playful, recreational activities. Acting as a leisure milieu is but one of the modern family's functions. Others include the reproduction and socialisation of children, and acting as a unit for economic consumption. Analytically it is possible to separate these functions, but in day-to-day living they are thoroughly interwoven. Since this is the case, is it not likely that any growth in leisure in society at large will have general consequences for *all* aspects of family life? Dumazedier invites us to regard leisure as a new basis for family solidarity, and also as a new threat in so far as individuals seek release from marital constraints to 'do their own things'. He also argues that family life in general is becoming leisurely in that choice of residence increasingly takes account of leisure opportunities, and that former chores including play with children and visiting relatives are being recultivated as leisure activities.[42] Marital partners are now self-selected on the basis of inter-personal attraction. Marriage for love is taken for granted, not a privilege reserved for chivalrous aristocrats. Men and women marry not out of a sense of religious duty or economic necessity. The main value sought in marriage is intimate companionship. Stripped of the language of romantic love, partners in mature marriages continue to name the quality of the conjugal relationship as the feature of family life valued above all others.[43] Sociologists have coined the term 'companionate marriage' to describe this ideal that so many contemporary couples seek.

Does this have anything at all to do with leisure? Is it not simply that the weakening of the extended family, the decline in fertility and the loss of some one-time family functions including economic production have heightened the importance of the conjugal relationship? Writers including Dumazedier insist on adding the growth of leisure with the value it places on choice and doing things for the instrinsic satisfaction as one reason why marriage has become essentially a matter of personal choice, dissoluble whenever the relationship fails to fulfil the partners' expectations. Kaplan agrees, and argues that the family has moved from its earlier 'legalistic, traditionalist and economic foundations to more amorphous, unpredictable, personal and cultural relationships'. Like Dumazedier, he believes that, 'Here lies its new dangers and also its new opportunities.'[44]

Sex has been claimed for the realm of play. Rather than a religious obligation, marital right or procreative duty, Foote argues that sex has become above all else an activity pursued for mutual pleasure, by men and women, in and outside marriage.[45] This could be a straightforward consequence of the emancipation of women, more effective contraception and the secularisation of knowledge about sexual drives and emotions. But could a 'fun morality' borne by the growth of leisure be another contributor? Martha Wolfenstein claims that a fun morality has transformed American parent–child relationships.[46] Instead of parents disciplining children into obedience, their relationships are now enlivend by fun. The infant is no longer treated as a dangerous savage whose instincts must be controlled, repressed if necessary, but as a being whose potential must be allowed full expression. Parents, grandparents even more so, often contrast today's free-and-easy childhoods with the stricter treatment they recall.[47] Children are now welcomed as a source of pleasure. Fathers hope sons will grow into mates, while mothers seek their daughters' friendship. These changes could be no more than the consequences of smaller families and the enlightenment spread by child psychology. Need any reference be made to a fun morality and leisure?

Writers who press leisure's claims point out that the growth of free time and disposable income have boosted recreational activity, and more besides. People have chosen to spend some of their increased leisure on their homes, in their families. Maybe life-styles offering pleasure in parenthood and conjugal companionship are more fulfilling than preoccupation with out-of-home recreation. If leisure is growing, then surely, it is argued, we must expect the character of family life to bear the imprint. Could the transformation of family life be one stage *en route* towards a 'society of leisure'?

7

LEISURE AND THE FUTURE

Since their subject's birth sociologists have been striving to glimpse the future. Some have now abandoned the effort, but the temptation remains as strong as ever. As in the nineteenth century, contemporary sociologists offer contrasting interpretations of history's course, but some otherwise diametrically opposed accounts converge on one conclusion: that leisure is going to play a much stronger role in our future lives than at present.

Previous chapters have hinted that such a future may beckon. Claims that leisure's effects on work and family life are mounting rest on the view that leisure's growth amounts to more than extra time and money for fun and games. Leisure is seen as playing not only a *larger* but also a *stronger* role in shaping our identities, life-styles and other institutions. These claims derive from broader interpretations of our society's trajectory. Even if it cannot end the argument, the study of leisure demands that these interpretations be brought to the foreground and exposed to critical scrutiny, which is the purpose of this chapter. The net effect of such exposure, in my view, is to diminish confidence that a 'society of leisure' awaits. While leisure has grown and largely escaped from determination by other institutions to make an increasingly independent contribution to life's quality, the case for leisure centrality is liable to crumble the moment it is systematically examined. But assessments of probable futures cannot be more than best estimates. No one can claim the last word. Everyone with sufficient interest is entitled to weigh the evidence and arguments, to form their own conclusions.

Post-industrialism: the optimistic prospectus

One optimistic school of thought foresees technology lightening the demands of work, while raising our living standards and simultaneously making the remaining work more satisfying. It envisages a growing proportion of all employment in the white-collar, tertiary, service sectors, in jobs requiring education and training, bestowing high status and income, and offering work that means more than the sale of labour power. It predicts the pace of change rendering rigid, authoritarian, rule-bound bureaucracies dysfunctional, and requiring their replacement by fluid, democratic organisations. We are invited to anticipate the lifetime career giving way to working lives that provide a variety of occupational experiences in discontinuous work roles. It is claimed that hours of work will decline while incomes and living standards rise, and that the remaining jobs will be leisurely, performed not primarily for extrinsic rewards but for the intrinsic satisfaction. As a result, it is argued, the division between work and the rest of life that arose with industrialism will dissolve, leading to a fusion of work and leisure. This scenario is rarely sketched in full. Commentators normally dwell on parts of the argument while taking others for granted. Considering the future of leisure not only allows but requires examination of the entire prospectus.

The changing shape of the occupational structure is the best rehearsed of all the optimists' arguments. Pre-industrial man had no alternative but to engage in *primary* economic activity. He met his needs by exploiting his habitat – the land and sea. Agriculture was the main occupation. The industrial era brought a growth of employment in a *secondary* manufacturing sector. People moved from the land into factories, where they transformed raw materials into useful goods. After a certain point, it is argued, manufacturing employment stabilises, then declines. In this sense the economy is de-industrialised. This is due to an 'industry effect' and an 'occupation effect'. The industry effect occurs as demand shifts from goods to health, education, financial and other services. The occupation effect occurs within industries. Scientific and technological developments combined with the prominence of large-scale enterprises reduce shop-floor employment while creating new armies of clerks, managers and technologists who service the direct producers. In the USA there are already more white-collar than industrial manual workers and Britain is destined to follow suit. Already, only 10 per cent of all workers are directly producing goods.[1] In time the manual working class will cease to be the mass of the people and become a minority. Irrespective of the validity of the *embourgeoisement* theory which claims that the remaining manual workers will become less proletarian in outlook, the growing proportion of jobs in the white-collar sector guarantees a middle-class majority, assuming that all other things stay equal.

Alongside this decline of traditional industrial employment, knowledge rather than physical capital becomes the key factor of production. Earlier generations of machines replaced human muscles. It is claimed that the new 'information technologies' are extending the capacity of the human brain. Skill, knowledge and brainpower, in one phrase 'human capital' becomes decisive for further economic development. Stonier predicts a future in which education will 'employ' 50 per cent of the 'workforce', either as teachers or students.[2] Alan Touraine envisages the emergence of a 'programmed society' in which the technocrats, the people with the knowledge required to make society tick, will be celebrated as the new high priests.[3] The analogy between society and the electronic computer is intentional.

Daniel Bell has written extensively on the post-industrial society, a phrase inspired by the decline of industrial work.[4] Alongside this trend, Bell believes that older forms of boss–worker conflict will recede in importance, and that the major political issues of the future will concern services such as health and education. These are the matters that are to become central to our interests, as workers and consumers. Paul Halmos envisages the growth of careers in education, health and welfare services creating a new service-oriented, professional class.[5] He believes that by virtue of their crucial roles, including the services rendered to other élite groups, the ethic of this new class could become the dominant ethos of our future society. In Halmos's view, we are going to become service-oriented and socio-psychologically sensitive rather than obsessed with economic growth and political power.

Fluidity is a key phrase in the optimists' scenario. We are told that the pace of technological change, an educated population and the emergence of multinational conglomerates pursuing multiple goals, co-operating with national governments to further social objectives in addition to seeking profits, will render traditional bureaucracies obsolete. Bennis argues that the 'turbulent' conditions of the post-industrial era will require 'democratic', decentralised organisations with loose, organic, flexible structures that allow full and free communication, and are integrated not by old-fashioned leadership but through consensus and influence based on technical competence.[6] He foresees even armies abandoning the 'military model' in favour of management as a process of co-ordination among experts who respect each others' skills, and who will be brought together temporarily as 'task forces' to address specific problems. Can we still afford to maintain authoritarian bureaucracies in which those who know, at the bottom, are denied the power to act, while those with the power, at the top, lack the necessary knowledge? Toffler has written provocatively on how we will all have to cope with *future shock*, the condition of finding that the societies for which we were socialised no longer exist.[7] Like Bennis, he predicts bureaucracy yielding to *adhocracy* with titles changing, responsibilities shifting, and organisation charts needing updating every few months. Future service workers, we are assured, will not be sentenced to careers in dull bureaucracies, but will work in exciting, turbulent and democratic organisations.

We are tempted with the prospect of fluidity extending into and reshaping our careers. The argument is that the pace of technological and occupational change will render the lifelong career as obsolete as rigid bureaucracy. Guest contemplates a division of the normal working life into three phases: the first using skill and knowledge acquired in education, the second in management and the third in routine administration.[8] But this scenario is only one of several possibilities. Retraining and re-education could become lifelong processes. Fred Best argues that the linear life plan of education–work–retirement has already become dysfunctional and advocates allowing individuals to choose between a variety of sequences.[9] Those wishing to retrain could spend sabbaticals in college, but there would be no compulsion. Best believes that this change, along with greater choice over weekly and annual work schedules, will enable men (and women) to gain control over the 'time of their lives'. Goldring predicts a future in which we will all become multipurpose men, performing a variety of jobs, and in addition to meeting the demands of occupational change, he believes that variety will resolve the problem of monotonous work.[10]

All told this package of developments is seen leading to satisfying working lives for all. For decades scholars have pondered whether the society of leisure will mean making twice as many pins in half the time, or only half as many in twice the time. Instead of acquiring more and more free time and income, could the resources generated by economic growth be employed to humanise work? Optimists assure us that this is on the horizon. Humane considerations and economic logic are to operate in unison. They point to growing resistance through strikes, sabotage and absenteeism to degradation by machines and bureaucracy, and draw attention to the managers and professional people who are opting out. Fred Best believes that the younger generation in particular is reluctant to accept routine work, and that women and formerly oppressed minorities will reject servile jobs.[11] He envisages an 'abundance society' in which the growth of education, welfare spending and consumer credit make the link between work and income increasingly tenuous, one result being that individuals will be persuaded to work only by the promise of intrinsic satisfactions. In the past trade unions have sought improved rewards *from* work. In the future it is envisaged that they will negotiate greater rewards *in* work. Once individuals realise that this is possible, it is argued, proposals for leisure in work will arouse all the ardour and solidarity traditionally associated with the working class.[12] Abrahamsson informs us that:

The increase in economic productivity in organisations and in society-at-large creates the possibility of reducing working hours, and consequently of gaining greater freedom to organise for the improvement of working conditions. Economic development also provides the basis for the improvement of education and culture. In turn these may become the foundation for a critique of existing productive relations, and for the rational and deliberate changing of these relations.[13]

Work is to become more satisfying and also, according to the scenario under discussion, less time-consuming. Technology and efficient, fluid organisations will ensure that we do not have to choose between pay and play; both will be delivered in greater quantities than ever. This prospect should not surprise us; it will involve only a continuation of past trends. Fred Best calculates that in the 'agricultural era' work accounted for 29 per cent of all lifetime, whereas in the USA by 1970 only 13.4 per cent of the population's lives were being spent at work.[14] Best sees no reason why, in the future, as in the past, machines should not take over an increasing proportion of society's work. He envisages a time when '... one person assisted by the decision-making and electronic activating resources of a computer may, for example, be able to operate and supervise an entire hydro-electric or oil refining plant'.[15] The silicon chip is presumably bringing this prospect ever nearer.

To enjoy this future, it is argued, one thing we must do is to revise some of our conventional ideas. We are advised to purge ourselves of any remnants of the old work ethic, the idea that work is virtuous and that all able-bodied people ought to be gainfully employed. It is argued that such values have become not only redundant, but positively injurious. If increasing numbers need not and, in many cases, will be unable to work, some writers urge acknowledgement of a 'right of leisure', and even insist that we legislate for 'the right not to work and still be considered a worthy human being'.[16]

The consummation of the above trends is to be a fusion of work and leisure as these spheres become increasingly similar. 'In the future we will see a fusion of work and play. Play will be our work, as it is for children. Work will be our play: we will demand the right to occupy ourselves with deeply fulfilling activities.'[17] The Central Policy Review Staff has argued that microcircuitry's implications for telecommunications will allow managers and professional employees to spend more working time at home, with teleconferences partly superseding travel, thereby helping to break down the previously clear division between work and the rest of life.[18] Stanley Parker predicts and advocates a fusion of work and leisure of the type we can already glimpse in the 'extension pattern' life-styles of individuals whose jobs are intrinsically satisfying.[19] Some would describe such a state as a 'society of leisure'. Is this really the shape of things to come?

The limits to growth: the pessimistic scenario

Ecological pessimists criticise the above forecasts.[20] They agree on the importance of placing the future on the agenda, but accuse 'orthodox' post-industrial theorists of intellectual conservatism, of remaining prisoners of the past and present. Their prospectus, it is argued, is anything but the bold and imaginative creation its supporters claim. Critics point out that many of its predictions do little more than extrapolate current trends with the result that beneath some novel terminology the future looks not too unlike the present.[21] Pessimists insist that the most important point about the future is that current trends simply cannot continue, and that there must be a radical break followed by genuinely novel developments.

The idea that history is approaching another threshold, comparable to the Industrial Revolution, was popularised by the Club of Rome, a think-tank of American academics and businessmen. The title of their report, *The Limits to Growth*, [22] summarises the argument. They portray industrial society under attack from three converging threats: population increase, the destruction of the environment and the exhaustion of finite, non-renewable material resources such as uranium, aluminium and the fossil fuels. The Club of Rome challenges mankind to recognise that there are ecological limits to growth, that at some point we will have to halt the march of industrialism and accept zero increases in consumption.

This scenario has been given repeated restatements. Miles has endeavoured to awaken his fellow Americans from their dream, and alert humanity to the impending ecological disaster, the inevitable sequel to continuing population growth, profligate use of limited energy resources and blind exploitation of land and sea which, he argues, are already stretching our social and political organisations to breaking point.[23] Miles believes that at some point in the not too distant future we must all accept simpler life-styles, and recognise that it is beyond mother earth's capacity to allow us all to live in the style to which America's upper-middle classes have grown accustomed.

Robert Heilbronner also believes that the business civilisation must be superseded.[24] It is not just that the growth of industry will eventually confront the limits of nature – the fact that the earth's resources are finite. Heilbronner believes we are hastening the day by polluting the environment in ways that may inflict uncomfortable climatic change. Tension between rich and poor nations, the squeeze on profits and the rise of planning are offered as signs that the business civilisation is reaching the end of its course. Heilbronner gives this epoch another century at the outside, and anticipates increasing strife for shares of finite resources inspiring a search for new goals and values.

These 'alarmist' predictions are contested by 'technological optimists' who accept that the earth's resources are finite, but draw attention to the fact that we are only just beginning to explore the wider universe, and believe that mankind's ingenuity will devise answers as the age of hydrocarbons closes. They point out that the latest technologies are more energy-efficient than their predecessors, insist there remains scope for bringing more land under cultivation, increasing soil fertility, reducing waste, exploiting geothermal, solar and wind power, and assure us that 'a desirable future is at least in the realm of the possible'.[25] Freeman and Jahoda believe that the best possible future from the point of view of averting international conflict and war over claims on inadequate resources, will combine greater equality between nations and *high* rates of economic growth.

Writers who believe that ecological calamity lies just around the corner quickly lose patience with technological optimists, and accuse them of encouraging a public indifference which allows politicians to take comfort in experts' disagreements. Sauvy insists that the growth of consumption *is* a very serious threat to humanity that will never be halted while nation states remain locked in economic competition.[26] He believes that salvation requires a world government to plan and allocate resources in a zero-growth era, and is alarmed by how few of the world's leaders are willing to face this necessity.

Sociologists are hardly qualified to arbitrate in controversies about physical limits and technological possibilities. Their main contribution has been to suggest that over and above whatever ecological limits we face, there are social barriers to the further development of industrial civilisation. According to Fred Hirsch,[27] *social limits to growth* are responsible for three contemporary problems: firstly the *paradox of affluence*, the fact that we persistently strive for growth despite professing disappointment with the results; secondly our *distributional compulsion*, our increasing anxiety about our 'shares of the cake'; and thirdly the *reluctant collectivism* that spreads as Left and Right propose new forms of state regulation despite their lip-service to individual liberty. While regretting the demise of freedom, we all seem driven to demand new forms of state intervention, whether to curb monopoly capital or trade unions. Hirsch argues that we can only understand the source of these problems once we recognise a *social element* in personal consumption. He distinguishes *material* and *positional* goods. With the latter our enjoyment diminishes if others also possess them. Fashionable clothes, motor cars and education are examples. The pleasures we derive are partly conditional upon others being denied access. Education opens life-chances only when given levels of qualification are the prerogative of minorities. Beaches and the countryside lose their attraction when invaded by the hordes. Hirsch argues that economic growth progressively shifts the balance of demand towards positional goods and services. In pay bargaining, therefore, we become increasingly aware of relativities rather than what our wages and salaries will actually buy. The net results are 'crush' and 'congestion' rather than serenity. 'If everyone stands on tiptoe, no one sees better.'[28] Hirsch believes that this frustration inspires our distributional compulsion which leads to the slide towards collectivism, and argues that the only answer is to embrace collectivism rationally, to narrow economic differentials thereby reducing competition for top jobs, salaries and educational credentials and to remove many goods and services from the market in favour of public allocation. In Hirsch's view, this is the only way of preserving certain residual areas for market forces and individual freedom.

Hirsch is but one of a body of writers who believes that social and cultural contradictions are driving our current civilisation to an impasse. The crux of the argument is that economic growth has ceased to accord with well-being, and that at some point we must set ourselves new objectives. Does a rising Gross National Product any longer indicate a real growth of living standards? Or does it mean only that we are laundering each other's dirty washing; handling the physical, psychological and social pollution from our very attempts to increase output? In certain cases official economic growth appears to mean only that we have professionalised services such as the care of children and the ageing that were previously performed through voluntary effort. Given this interpretation of mankind's predicament, worker resistance to monotonous jobs and attacks on diseconomies of scale are read as signs of a public prepared to respond to new values. The end of political weakness in the Third World, which will make the oil crises of the 1970's mere foretastes of the future, could accentuate the search for escape routes.

How will change occur? It is no longer fashionable to believe that the future is determined by iron laws of history and will be built by blind socio-economic forces. Ecological pessimists comfort us with the thought that we can create a brighter future, and will be motivated to do so once we have diagnosed the sources of our frustrations. It is argued that the impending impasse will prove a fertile ground for radical change ideologies. Popular discontent is expected to fuse with the radical visions of the future that intellectuals are beginning to offer, fomenting social movements leading to a break with industrial society, as traumatic as the birth of industrial civilisation itself. Tiryakian juxtaposes two modern conceptions of time.[29] The first sees history as *progress* – a steady long-term upgrading. This concept of time, Tiryakian believes, corresponded with the experience of the nineteenth-century middle classes, and sections of the twentieth-century's working class, whereas today it is increasingly 'seen through' as a myth. Tiryakian's second conception of time is apocalyptic and conceives history as a series of totally disrupting, abrupt and sometimes violent changes which will be repeated in the future. This imagery has a long religious history, but Tiryakian draws attention to its recent appearance in secular forms appealing to the middle classes in addition to oppressed and peripheral groups. He believes the resurgence of this conception of historical time is related to a growing awareness of the impending population, ecological and nuclear time bombs. Once people are convinced that salvation will be confined to the prepared, it is argued, visions of a radically new social order will act as catalysts, helping to end the industrial era. This is where theories of leisure re-enter the scenario. Prospectuses that enable men to understand how play can offer fulfilment, that show how achievement can mean something other than hard work and occupational success, may entice mankind to abandon the business civilisation's goals and values.

Ivan Illich is among those who would welcome the transformation. His stated intention is to undermine confidence in industrialism and its professions, thereby helping to precipitate radical change. He indicts industrialism for creating a 'modernised poverty', a 'disabling enrichment' with which we 'mutilate' and 'paralyse' ourselves through depending on mass-produced goods and services that destroy our power to act creatively and autonomously. Instead of relying on 'disabling professions' – doctors, scientists, teachers and social workers – Illich advocates 'conviviality', an austere modern existence that will confer liberties rather than rights, with men directly and personally shaping and satisfying an expanding proportion of their needs. Illich insists that useful work need not be employment. Indeed, he argues, unemployment has become a condition for genuinely useful, autonomous work.[30]

The society of leisure

Writers who envisage a 'society of leisure' are neither predicting nor prescribing a life devoted entirely to fun and games. Everyone realises that there is going to remain more to life than leisure. The phrase 'society of leisure' is a conceptual equivalent to 'industrial society'. Industrial work never accounted for the greater part of lifetime, but its claims were once considerable, and the rest of life was organised around the demands of industrial employment. Talk of a society of leisure is based on the expectation that the growth of leisure time will continue and, moreover, that our leisure interests and values will play the central role in our life-styles once commanded by work in industry. It envisages the growth of leisure amounting to more than a few extra weeks vacation plus additional cash for alcohol and sports gear. Social structural changes of a 'revolutionary' character are anticipated either as a result of current technological, economic and occupational trends continuing to unfold, or as a consequence of industrialism grinding itself to a halt. Leisure is sometimes offered as a catalyst whose values will help reshape the social order, otherwise as an inevitable beneficiary of the impending changes.

Earlier chapters have discussed how uses of leisure are shaped by individuals' jobs and domestic roles, but have also drawn attention to arguments about the autonomy of leisure and, indeed, to ways in which, certain writers claim, leisure now exerts an influence across these other spheres. Forecasts of a society of leisure treat these 'straws in the wind' as pointers to a time when leisure will become our main arena for identity formation, status aquisition and bestowing meaning on life. According to Newman:

Undeniably the significance of work has universally receded into the background, and centrality in the formation of self-definition has passed within the compass of the non-occupational sphere, with leisure outstandingly the single most dominant element. It is in his leisure activity that late-industrial man satisfies his needs to feel adequate, derives his ego identification, and achieves skills instrumental towards social integration, possibly to the extent of even infusing meaningful content to objectively dull and monotonous work.[31]

Some writers argue that anyone seeking a clear statement of contemporary society's values should look not to traditional religion, or to the pronouncements of politicians and captains of industry, but to our uses of leisure. Inglis names sport as the people's religion in an otherwise secular age which expresses the values we cherish.[32] MacCannell claims tourism as the religion of contemporary man; a ritual that celebrates the differentiation of society, through which men strive for transcendence of the totality and attempt to incorporate its fragments into a unified experience.[33] He argues that this role of tourism has been created during the transition from industrial to 'modern' society, in which life-styles replace occupations as our prime sources of social relationships, status and action, where creativity falls almost exclusively in the province of cultural rather than industrial production and where people seek intimacy and spontaneity away from work.

Joffre Dumazedier, the French sociologist and leading European apostle of the society of leisure, argues that leisure is fast becoming the central element in people's lives, the basis for self-identity and consciousness, overwhelming traditional forms of class awareness.[34] In the future, Dumazedier believes, our most keenly felt privations will involve our capacities to develop and practise preferred leisure interests. As work is invaded by leisure values, Dumazedier argues, people will not rest content with music while they work and company sports facilities, but will demand interesting jobs, decent conditions and congenial social relations. In the USA Max Kaplan has been a consistent spokesman on leisure's growing importance. He argues that leisure has already become much more than a means of recuperation,[35] and that our progress towards a 'cultivated order' depends upon learning to use leisure to maximum benefit.[36] According to both Kaplan and Dumazedier, contemporary mankind in general, and political leaders in particular, need to be alerted to the new priorities. It is no longer sufficient, they claim, that facilities for sport and the arts, education and urban planning should be tuned to economic growth and servicing the work-force: our social policies need to allow a civilisation of leisure to flourish. John Nisbet has drawn educators' attention to the new role of leisure:

Freud described adolescence as a period when the individual makes two important adjustments in the transition to adult life, adjustment to sex and adjustment to work. Nowadays we may have to add a third – adjustment to leisure. This is not only because of the shadow of unemployment which hangs over many school-leavers. Leisure is an important part of our lives. For many people, leisure time is the real part of life – when they are most truly themselves – as Aristotle said.[37]

If we want to solve problems of conflict, alienation, anomie, extend democracy and supply meaning to life, should we now be looking to leisure rather than conventional politics and work? John Haworth offers leisure as a theatre through which to stimulate community involvement and development, and to provide individuals with opportunities to create their own experiences and futures.[38] Similar claims have been made for 'community art'.[39] Haworth advocates public participation in recreation planning, management and research. He admits that such participation will be lengthy and costly, and that vocal action groups may sometimes prove unrepresentative. But he nevertheless presses the case for participation, and not only as a means to efficiency in recreation management by ensuring that real needs are met and stimulating self-help. Haworth believes that by involving communities in creating their own leisure opportunities we can become a more democratic society in which individuals are able to fulfil their creative potential. In the past such proposals would have been dubbed 'palliatives'. Does this reaction still carry conviction? Or has leisure become the heart of the matter; a major contributor to individual well-being, to the quality of inter-personal relationships, and to the 'health' of society in general?

Many mainstream sociologists find it difficult to take these questions seriously. Could this be because their discipline is still living in the past? Politics, the economy and stratification have always been the prestigious specialisms. It is easy to understand why. Sociology was born in the nineteenth century in attempts to explain the changes being wrought by industrialism. Through the debates and with the concepts forged by their discipline's founders, later generations of sociologists have been well equipped to set the present in the context of the immediate past; in the context of the transformations associated with the advent and development of industrialism. But if we want to think not backwards but forwards, from the present into the future, which is what the classical sociologists themselves accomplished, we may need to recast sociology's terms of debate. It could be that areas of life of subsidiary importance in industrial society, and therefore rightly relegated to secondary status within sociology, are going to assume renewed significance. Pronovost proclaims leisure as one such area, and draws an analogy between contemporary theories of leisure and classic sociological theories. 'The leisure sciences constitute one of the instruments that industrial societies have developed to better understand themselves. This phenomenon is probably analogous to that which led to the birth of sociology in the nineteenth century.'[40] How seriously we treat this claim will depend on the credence lent to forecasts that the near future will belong to a society of leisure.

The society with leisure

Leisure might appear a splendid each-way bet. Whether present trends continue or exhaust themselves, the scenarios sketched earlier promise that leisure will inherit the future. A useful warning before joining the bandwagon is that few present-day social scientists believe that the future is fully determined. Predictions are choices, never more than best estimates from a range of possibilities. Which course history eventually takes may depend on unforeseen, perhaps unforeseeable circumstances.

Some writers, the 'moderates', argue that the role of leisure throughout the foreseeable future will look more like the present than either the limits to growth or optimistic scenarios suggest; that leisure may well continue to grow, but is unlikely to stray beyond its present role. It is argued that flamboyant optimistic and pessimistic forecasts both exaggerate the pace of change. Are current trends really likely to deliver a society of leisure, or race us to an impasse from which a radically different social order will emerge?

Perrow notes that the automated factory, whose arrival has been predicted since the 1950s, is still confined to the realm of ideas rather than bricks and mortar.[41] Fred Best says it is possible, but is it at all probable that before long entire hydroelectric plants and oil refineries will be supervised by solitary workers? As for the multiplication of fulfilling, service occupations, Levison reminds us that the tertiary sector includes cooks and cleaners in addition to welfare professions, and that white-collar jobs are not always brimful of intrinsic satisfactions.[42] Rather than widening opportunities for autonomous and interesting employment, some argue that current trends are routinising managerial and professional jobs.

Are bureaucracies really on the verge of collapse? How many employees now operate as members of self-managing task forces? Far from decentralising power, technological innovations, especially the computer, appear more likely to facilitate centralisation of key decisions.[43] If we remain this side of the ecological impasse, is there any convincing reason to expect the character of work to change? The logic of a market economy obliges enterprises to organise their affairs to maximise output and minimise costs.[44] Is organising work to increase intrinsic satisfactions a genuine option? Communist economies exhibit similar priorities to capitalist nations. The behaviour of workers throughout the world suggests that high incomes and standards of consumption are valued above humanising work itself. Where are radical change ideologies taking root? Sustaining motivation on monotonous assembly lines is a problem, but it is not yet forcing car manufacturers to satisfy the mass market with alternative technologies. It is possible to locate young and middle-aged, working- and middle-class drop-outs, but many more seem to be fighting to opt into higher education and the 'rat race'.

Moderates find numerous grounds to challenge forecasts of work becoming leisurely. And even if it occurred, the fusion of work and leisure might prove less attractive than optimists make it sound. The self-employed dealers who arrange Tupperware parties tend to be successful only while this fusion lasts. Once they exhaust their circles of friends and begin selling to strangers (who spend less), many quickly desert the occupation.[45] The Tupperware organisation benefits from using leisure circles as marketing networks, but whether the dealers' life-styles are more fulfilling than those individuals whose leisure can be insulated from commercial pressures is less self-evident.

Sceptics treat forecasts of a collapse of work as wishful thinking, like its imminent humanisation. During the 1970s unemployment returned to the agenda of social issues, and we were alerted to the silicon chip revolution. But everyone who has carefully examined the trends and forces in operation expresses reservations about the collapse of work theory. In 1980 there were more people in jobs than in 1970. The growth of unemployment did not result from a net loss of jobs, but was the consequence of the labour force growing even more quickly than the demand for labour. As explained in Chapter 3, for people in employment hours of work are not declining rapidly. During the 30 years following the Second World War, the average workweek for Britain's manual workers was trimmed by only three hours. The standard work-week contracted more rapidly than actual hours worked. Grass-roots demands for 35-hour workweeks rest largely on hopes of overtime instead of basic rates for the same number of hours as formerly. On average, present-day citizens spend *more* hours at work during their lifetimes than their great-grandparents.[46] Hours worked per year while in the labour force have declined, but the fall in mortality has length-

ened the typical citizen's working life. There has been no collapse, and rather than even a decline of work it is strictly correct
to talk only of containment. Lifetime has increased, and leisure
time has grown not so much at the expense of, as alongside and
more rapidly than working time. This 'new' work-free lifetime
has enlarged the sections of the population outside the work-
force, mainly the young and retired.[47] The annual demands upon the typical worker have lightened, but only marginally. For
women the trend has been towards spending a greater part of the
life span in employment. Between 1961 and 1975, for men the
trends were towards less paid employment but greater involvement in housework. For women the trends ran in the opposite
direction.[48] Overall there was a 10 per cent decline in domestic
and paid working time. The continuing historical trend is towards more leisure. But the current pace of change offers little
support to predictions of work becoming an almost incidental
pastime.

What about the silicon chip? Will it mean 'enforced leisure'?
Another school of thought maintains that microcircuitry and
automation will not reduce but simply change the pattern of
employment.[49] A common mistake is to imagine that there is a
finite amount of work to be done, and that as machines perform
more, humans must do less. This theory about the implications
of technological change is well worn; it can be traced to the Lud-
dites. In practice technological progress has always led to rising
standards of living, a growth in spending power, demand for
new goods and services and a net increase in employment. Industrial economies are inherently dynamic. Some jobs do dis-
appear, maybe half the starters in manufacturing industry during any normal 10-year period. But in the past, the slack has
been more than compensated. In the 1960s there were forecasts
of computers driving managers and clerical workers into idleness, but employment in these sectors actually increased. Computers replaced 1650 clerks who formerly maintained unemployment benefit records, but 450 new computer jobs were created,
and total employment administering social security rose, with
new areas of work being opened up for staff released by the
computer.[50] New products whose mass production has been
made commercially viable by microprocessors include television

games, digital watches and pocket calculators. Before long, voice-operated typewriters are expected on the market. Word processors can displace over 50 per cent of the typists previously required, but they also create a demand for new types of work that were formerly impossible or unprofitable, such as advertising by standard letter.

New jobs are not created by blind technological forces. They are born through political decisions and business initiative. The point at issue, however, is that mankind's appetite for new products looks anything but quenched. One white-collar union estimated in 1978 the word processors would replace a quarter of a million office workers by 1983;[51] a significant loss, but not of a size to render reabsorption inconceivable. Burck argues that the movement into labour intensive occupations such as teaching, medicine and social work, where productivity is static if not declining, will make it increasingly difficult in the future to release any lifetime from employment.[52]

If jobs are on offer, there is little evidence that people of working age will exercise a preference for leisure time. Surveys generally find that higher income is still the stronger demand.[53] Complaints of work interfering with leisure are common only among the 'harried leisure class': individuals in well-paid and time-consuming professional and managerial jobs.[54] Why anticipate a mass exodus from the 'rat race'? Maybe it is better to be prosperous and harried than poor. In 1973 Young and Willmott cautiously estimated that annual hours of work would be trimmed by 13 per cent before the end of the century.[55] This could hardly be described as a collapse of work, and in the past even cautious forecasts have proved exaggerated. In 1963 Faunce envisaged the four-day week becoming the norm within 25 years.[56] The four-day week is spreading, but more slowly than Faunce anticipated.[57]

Rather than material needs approaching fulfilment, 'moderates' insist that the evidence from the most affluent societies suggests mankind's material wants are capable of indefinite extension. Gershuny has drawn attention to the fact that the service occupations where employment is increasing most rapidly are not offering the personal services whose ethos Halmos expects to spread, but services for manufacturing industry, as provided, for example, by architects, financial institutions and personnel departments.[58] As the economy becomes more capital intensive, real wage and salary levels increase, thereby raising the relative costs of labour-intensive services, including the performing arts, where it is impossible to replace humans with machinery. This is why, Gershuny argues, even senior managers today find it 'pays' to take time off work to paint their houses and repair their cars instead of purchasing the services. The real trend, Gershuny claims, is not towards a personal service society but a self-service economy. Demand has risen for durable consumer goods; household capital, that families service themselves. Hence the spread of do-it-yourself stores. Households buy the tools and materials to do their own self-servicing instead of hiring the prohibitively expensive labour of service workers. If Gershuny's analysis is correct, a motor car designed with a view to owner-servicing should find a waiting market. But in the context of the present discussion, the implication of Gershuny's portrait of the emergent self-service economy is that any time released from paid employment is more likely to be absorbed by domestic 'work' than leisure.

My 'best estimate' is that the 'moderates' have the balance of probability of their side. The post-industrial optimists', or ecological-limits, scenarios may dawn, but for the present it seems unwise to ask or expect too much of leisure. The chances are that leisure will not solve our problems of work and democracy, or supply meaning and fulfilment to otherwise empty lives. There are dangers of overselling leisure. Overall there has been a growth of leisure, which must have enhanced its ability to influence our behaviour and values in other spheres. It is not difficult to find real-life illustrations of leisure-centred life-styles. But the extent to which identities anchored in leisure are liable to spill across life in general appears to vary greatly depending on age and occupational status.

Young people who have yet to establish their 'selves' in occupations and whose family involvements are minimal may adopt leisure interests which become major sources of identity and social intercourse. But this will not necessarily hold for individuals who have learnt to think of themselves as barristers and engineers, and whose time and income are committed by family responsibilities. Their leisure seems likely to remain an extension of work or domestic roles, and talk of using leisure to enrich their entire life-styles will continue to trivialise their domestic and occupational problems.

By now we should be aware of the pitfalls in attempting to generalise from experience and studies of young people at leisure. For decades commentators have scanned the youth culture believing they might discover signs of society's future within the lives and thoughts of the younger generation. Self-made man was followed by corporation man, and at the beginning of the 1970s Charles Reich applauded the era's student movement with its belief in 'self' and 'community' as the basis for a new consciousness, spreading throughout society, 'greening' America, and introducing a new social order.[59] In 1972 R. V. Speck wrote about the communes of the young, explained how drugs were used to gain new experiences and forecast the replacement of older styles of family life by loosely structured networks.[60] Sober commentators have always recognised the fragile foothold of 'way-out' life-styles, even among the young,[61] and have questioned whether adolescent values are capable of hosting a permanent way of life.[62] Young workers with money and the freedom it confers, but no families or 'places' of their own, are involved in a perpetual quest for 'territory' in youth clubs and discos, on the streets and soccer terraces. Changes in the division of labour by gender are encouraging girls to reject apprenticeships as 'household mums'. Like boys, they now congregate in their own peer groups, later in heterosexual crowds. Some of the most exciting events in these young people's lives involve venturing beyond known places to 'away' football grounds and city-centre discos to encounter strangers, though with friends close by. The settings are perfect for acting out exciting identities.[63] But is there any chance of such life-styles outlasting adolescence? The hippies of the 1960s suffered the fate of the Teddy boys and have been claimed by conventional marriages and careers. In the event of a collapse of paid employment and household work, so that occupational and domestic roles were unable to supply meaning and fill time on any scale resembling the past, then a scope and need could arise for an unprecedented commitment to leisure. But is this the most probable of all possible futures?

Moderates' visions do not dismiss leisure as trivial. They acknowledge that leisure has grown and will probably continue to do so – slowly. Our problem, they argue, will be to learn to live *with* leisure, but not in a society *of* leisure. They accept that it is no longer entirely secondary, but do not anticipate leisure becoming the pivot of our whole way of life. In the 1950s David Reisman wrote of the need to strike a new balance between work and leisure.[64] He believed people were becoming too educated to find interest in work, but inappropriately educated to derive interest from leisure. The challenge, in Reisman's view, was to reorganise work to make life, including leisure, more meaningful. A development that even moderates admit is towards people acquiring more choice over *when* to work. This is an international trend.[65] Firms are adopting schedules that fit their own needs rather than convention, and are allowing employees similar scope.[66] Work may not be subordinated to leisure or reshaped by leisure values, but the growth of non-working time is giving people more discretion to integrate their various roles and responsibilities to sustain preferred life-styles.

Leisure is not abolishing the age-old economic problem of scarcity. Individuals still have to choose between different values, and balance often conflicting pressures. They have to organise their time, balance their budgets and cope with the competition for 'positional' goods. More discretionary time and money mean more decisions, and therefore pressure. But maybe these are better described as *growing problems* rather than *limits to growth*. Individuals have to learn to balance the expressive, sometimes hedonistic, consumer values promoted by the leisure industries, against the work values these same corporations endeavour to enforce upon employees.[67] Leisure brings new pressures and problems, and also new opportunities. Murphy rejects the 'spare-time' concept as understating the contemporary role of leisure, and argues the case for treating leisure as a 'state of being', like 'love'. But he recognises that the rhythm of life imposed by industrialism is not going to evaporate, and that individuals' attempts to be 'at leisure' will continue to occur mainly in 'leisure time'.[68]

The society with leisure will retain all the complexities of the present, and is incapable of portrayal in the decisive strokes with which post-industrialism and the ecological impasse have been painted. Yet in certain respects the options moderates offer involve the clearer breaks with conventional modes of thought. For example, conventional and allegedly radical reappraisals of work share a surprising amount in common. Post-industrial and limits-to-growth spokesmen share the old Protestant ethic's assumption that work ought to be fulfilling. Critics and defenders of capitalism have also shared this ideology of work.[69] It is the society *with* leisure that suggests the possibility of a genuine reappraisal. It may be more realistic to accept that many jobs are boring, are likely to remain so, and that many workers will continue to be motivated primarily by extrinsic rewards. Although only a part of life, leisure may offer enough opportunity for fulfilment to make instrumental goals sufficient reason for working.

8

POLICIES FOR LEISURE

Leisure is an intellectual challenge to academics seeking to identify its character, sources and consequences. Is it also a social problem? Must public-spirited commentators do anything more than applaud the tides of change, then leave individuals to employ their leisure however they wish? As stated in this book's opening paragraphs, writers on leisure have rarely professed only academic interest. They have mostly concurred that leisure poses problems which become increasingly acute the more leisure grows. There have been strongly opposed views on the nature of the 'leisure problem', but writers have been virtually unanimous in pressing their subject's claims, demanding that the 'powers that be' recognise leisure's importance, expand provision and ensure that facilities of the right type are available. The following passages are different: they do not call for an urgent strengthening of the public leisure services. This is because the evidence from previous chapters is taken seriously. Among other things, it resists the definition of leisure as a problem, and questions the credibility of all official attempts to define the types of provision that will best serve the public's interests.

Paternalism

Our most familiar definitions of the leisure problem are explicitly paternal. They aim to inhibit sin and encourage virtue. The crux of the problem is seen as rising from people's inability to use their leisure time and money wisely. Give people too much free time, we are told, and they will be stranded in a wasteland, bored and apathetic, twiddling their thumbs wondering what to do. Alternatively they may misuse their leisure, harming others in addition to themselves. They may be tempted by drink, gambling, drugs and sexual promiscuity. Many writers have subscribed to the belief that the devil makes work for idle hands. In 1930 the authors of the *New Survey of London Life and Labour*[1] were arguing that numerous social problems including drink, sex and gambling stemmed from a lack of healthy leisure interests. Youth organisations were charged with a major responsibility for averting these pathologies.

According to this definition of the problem, salvation depends on the wise and cultured curbing undesirable uses of leisure, and guiding the masses towards worthwhile pastimes. Legislation has been demanded, and enacted, to limit opportunities to drink, gamble, and peruse pornographic films and magazines. Children and young people have normally been regarded as in special need of protection. Fiscal measures have been advocated to reinforce the law; taxes on drink, and subsidies for edifying activities such as opera, ballet and participant sport, for in addition to penalising sin, paternalists have supported the active promotion of innocuous or, better still, meritorious uses of leisure. Schools and youth organisations have been urged to spread the artistic and literary heritage, and to awaken interest in outdoor pursuits which, many have believed, are character-forming as well as healthy.

The case for sports and leisure centres is still occasionally argued in terms of keeping young people off the streets and out of trouble. Outbreaks of soccer hooliganism and street crime can be relied upon to inspire calls for better recreation facilities in the inner cities. But the heyday of paternalism has passed. Its critics have lost confidence in their ability to raise the level of popular culture. 'Vandals' have proved capable of ignoring youth clubs and sports centres, and even of inflicting their delinquent habits on these facilities. In the nineteenth century it was confidently hoped that mass education would civilise the people, spread high culture and nurture a God-fearing, church-attending nation. These aspirations have been confounded. We have learnt that however imaginative the promotion, the public remains capable of ignoring the claims of classical music and evening classes. People persistently use the freedom that leisure confers to avoid edifying, worthwhile, fulfilling, temperate pastimes.

This is not the only reason why paternalism has become unfashionable. 'We', the articulate opinion-forming strata who teach, write and read books, and legislate have suffered an even more basic loss of confidence. Until the Second World War there was no shortage of writers who would declare which uses of leisure were good for people. Today even the recreation professions are uncertain. They are in good company. The previous chapters have not supplied any clear answers. The rise of social science has made it necessary to base judgements on evidence. Even opponents of pornography are now asked to furnish proof of harm. If we cannot demonstrate that concerts and art galleries increase happiness, their case for support flounders. Hence the predicament of paternalists. Definitions of the leisure problem have been overhauled.

The liberal analysis

Travis has noted that, 'Leisure Services Planning and Management literature of the period 1935 to 1975 differs notably in content from the literature of the post-1975 period. The shift has taken place from viewing provisions as though they were for a unitary society, through to one which recognises that there are conflicting needs, conflicting and different groups, all competing for limited available resources.'[2] Paternalism has yielded ground to a liberal definition of the leisure problem which professes agnosticism as to which pastimes are particularly worthy. It makes a virtue of our inability to prescribe 'wholesome' recreations, arguing that we inhabit a plural society with a variety of age, ethnic, sex, regional and social class divisions which create a bewildering variety of 'taste publics', none of which comprise the mass of the people. What is required, it is argued, is not the imposition of any one set of 'correct' tastes, but the encouragement of diversity. The aims of public provision are cast in terms of assisting people to express whatever their interests happen to be, thereby developing their 'selves', and fulfilling potential that is frustrated in other spheres.

The élitist styles of still entrenched protectors of 'standards' and 'the heritage' have been exposed to vociferous criticism. The Arts Council now stands accused of being London-biased, arrogant, self-legitimising, and promoting just one definition of art. It has been castigated for ignoring the arts of Britain's ethnic minorities, and the community arts movement.[3] Why should the northern working class subsidise Covent Garden? Liberals demand that popular taste, not conventional standards of propriety, be the litmus test when allocating public resources.

Today's liberals rarely espouse extreme *laissez-faire* doctrines: that the pursuit of the good life requires no more than setting the people free from legal and financial restraints. The growth of leisure is seen as creating new problems that require collective solutions before individuals can be left free to pursue their interests. The age of leisure, it is argued, will not be an epoch of tranquillity, but will bring new kinds of scarcity and conflict. In the post-industrial society, older divisions, as between workers and bosses, may decline in importance, but new patterns of strife are anticipated. In the countryside the growth of leisure produces conflicts between agriculture, conservation and recreation, between different leisure interests such as angling and water-skiing, and between local residents and those seeking second homes. It is argued that allowing all citizens to pursue their interests requires management and planning, though not with the object of imposing any one set of approved pastimes. Quite the reserve: liberals advocate planning for leisure to create maximum scope for as many taste publics as possible to pursue their diverse interests without interfering with each other's enjoyment.

Education for leisure is proposed, not to sponsor approved recreation, but to widen young people's horizons. Schools are advised to introduce pupils not only to classical music, but also to jazz, rock and soul, and to the widest possible range of minority sports in addition to traditional team games. Liberals favour 'flexibility' and 'responsiveness' in the public leisure services. They aim not to direct, but to 'facilitate' all sections of the public in pursuing their interests. User-participation in management and planning, whether through opinion polls or representation on management committees, earns applause from today's liberals. They prefer 'cultural democracy', awakening the artistic creativity of the millions, to the 'democratisation of culture', taking traditional high culture to the masses. Detached youth workers and other *animateurs* who assist individuals and groups to identify and pursue whatever happens to interest them are also welcomed. Solutions to problems that are accentuated by leisure's growth are sought by channelling *resources*, not people, to cater for the widest possible array of tastes, improving *delivery* by making individuals aware of their opportunities and educating people to recognise the full range of their capacities and interests. Rather than moulding mass leisure into any prescribed pattern, liberals propose to cater for diversity, then leave an educated and informed public to make its own choices. They will admit that this agenda will prove more expensive than sponsoring selected pastimes and prohibiting others.

Rationalisation

Texts and conferences on the role of leisure continue to echo with pleas for more resources. The recreation professions and interested academics, whatever their disciplines, mostly unite in agreement that leisure is still undervalued by governments, and in education. However, in recent years the claims of leisure have been conceded in many corridors of power. In 1973 a House of Lords Select Committee, not a fringe pressure group, was arguing that, 'Until leisure has been accepted as an essential ingredient of life there will be no satisfactory provision of recreational facilities. Provision for recreation must be treated as a social service.'[4] Departments under Leisure and Recreation Services, and similar titles, have been established throughout local government. During the decade up to 1978 there was a five-fold increase, though with a depreciating currency, in public spending on recreation.[5] The leisure lobby has been winning its argument. Today leisure *is* generally recognised as part of the fabric of our social services.[6]

The current crusade is not just for yet additional resources, but for greater rationality in their distribution. Dispensers of public patronage are urged to be liberal in outlook and rational in method. Many students of public administration are appalled by the fragmented organisation of the public leisure services. An inevitable consequence, it is claimed, is that provision discords with people's needs. This complaint has arisen on both sides of the Atlantic. In America[7] and Britain public leisure facilities initially appeared for a variety of reasons – conservation, health and preserving historic landmarks, in addition to recreation. The leisure services developed 'incrementally'[8] through odd initiatives, at odd times, serving diverse ends. The legacy is an untidy patchwork with a multiplicity of public bodies supporting parks, community centres, playing fields, the arts and countryside recreation, and an absence of any overall policy for leisure with definite goals and priorities. Neither central nor local governments make comprehensive appraisals of leisure and attempt to create co-ordinated systems of leisure services. No British government has ever addressed a 'leisure problem'. Different government departments tackle a series of youth, educational, sport and arts problems.[9] Responsibilities for leisure are dispersed among 7 Secretaries of State, 10 central government departments, 17 other central government bodies, 9 types of regional authority, and five varieties of local government.[10] Critics protest that the inevitable outcomes include gaps, overlaps and inconsistencies. Many local authorities run their leisure services without even defining objectives. Provisions are maintained for 'traditional' reasons. Costs and benefits may never be appraised.[11] How much per player-match does it cost to maintain a cricket field? Few recreation departments are able to give precise answers to such questions. They are often surprised when calculations are made. Twenty pounds per head per match is not an unusual cost of cricket. When outcomes meet needs, critics argue it is through good fortune rather than efficient administration.

'Muddling through' offends the new generation of public administrators who believe in planning, systems analysis and management by objectives. Many would like a *rational* system of leisure administration to take an overall view of the public's leisure interests, to determine which can be met through the market and voluntary effort and to co-ordinate public services to fill gaps either with their own facilities, or by supporting other bodies. One partnership that advocates of rational policy-making and administration favour is between researchers and practitioners. The former are to establish the knowledge base, charting the public's interests, from which policies and provisions will follow. Should sociology accept this proposal? Some sociologists of leisure have flirted with practitioners. Others, myself included,[12] insist that their discipline forbids any closer relationship.

Leisure as social control

Earlier chapters have introduced elements of a theory which argues that far from allowing self-expression and fulfilment, leisure is best understood as a process of social control, and its providers as servants of power. We encountered this theory in Chapter 3 when surveying the growth of the leisure industries, and again in Chapters 5 and 6 when considering how uses of leisure are influenced by other social statuses. This 'class domination' theory[13] contends that the leisure concept is analytically arid but ideologically potent. Sociology's task is defined as criticising rather than adopting everyday ideas about leisure. These everyday ideas suggest that non-working time is free, and that its enjoyment is both proper and sufficient reward for working, though in fact, it is argued, uses of leisure are constrained by other social roles, particularly 'work' roles in the formal and domestic economies. The potency claimed for this ideology stems from its ability to define crime, boredom and other maladies as 'leisure problems', and thereby deflect discontents from challenging economic and political structures. According to this theory, leisure is the 'site' where labour power is reproduced and simultaneously threatened by hedonistic values which could undermine work discipline.[14] Hence the need overtly to praise leisure's freedom, while covertly controlling its uses which, it is claimed, has been the historic role of public provision. It is argued that the public's appetites are channelled towards forms of recreation which convey middle-class values, though presented in other guises, and foster qualities consistent with the ability and will to work including physical fitness, self-control, industriousness and team-spirit.[15] Any middle-class bias in the arts that receive public patronage is seen as inevitable rather than fortuitous; just one example of the cultural imperialism that characterises leisure in general.

Writers who develop this critique insist that leisure can offer no real solutions to life's problems. Rather than forging a partnership with practitioners, they seek to expose the social structural reality of leisure, and the true role of its services. They see little point in better provision. The main problems of our time, it is argued, are rooted in wider economic and political conditions. By exposing the ideology, and revealing the reality of leisure as currently serviced, its critics hope to remove one of the *status quo's* ideological supports, and thereby help to precipitate radical change.

Previous chapters have treated this theory unsympathetically. They have argued that uses of leisure are influenced but not rigidly determined by other statuses; that leisure does not *merely* reflect wider social structural constraints. They have insisted that attempts to control the people's pastimes have never been more than one side of a leisure dialectic. It is not difficult to quote examples of efforts to shape popular recreation to promote virtue, and generate profit, but the failures have been as impressive as the successes. The majority of the public have declined many offerings including evening classes, and used others, including soccer and vacations, for their own ends. Leisure styles have been influenced, but never dictated by multinationals and leisure services departments. Indeed, the providers have often found themselves at the mercy of consumers with fickle, apparently unpredictable, tastes. Evidence will be summarised below showing that leisure does not stifle grievances but makes an independent and positive contribution to our quality of life. It could be the radical critics, not the concept of leisure, who cast the ideological smoke-screen when they read satisfactions claimed from recreation as evidence of exploitation and oppression. If leisure makes life including work tolerable, and if it enables some people to live with grievances that might otherwise challenge political and economic structures, must it necessarily follow that the balance of deprivations and satisfactions available in our society-with-leisure negates the true interests of the public? Why dismiss as ideological the belief that leisure can make life tolerable, even enjoyable? Critics of leisure and its industries lie open to the charge of substituting their own ideology for consumers' preferences and interests when framing their arguments.[16]

Viewing leisure as a form of social control may be misleadingly one-sided, but this does not allow us to dismiss completely all the theory's propositions. If tastes are susceptible to *some* influence from 'above', an implication is that servicing the public's manifest interests could prove less liberal than its advocates suggest. Can we equate what people say, either on street corners or in survey interviews, with their 'real' interest? Will authentic interests always be consistent with manifest behaviour? Constraints rooted in other social roles may not script all the details of leisure, but individuals can express themselves only within whatever material and ideological constraints are operative.

It is surely deceitful to pretend that if only people will articulate their wants, whether in bingo or world cruises, some branch of the leisure industries will deliver the goods. People's leisure interests are so numerous and capable of such indefinite extension that not even the most benevolent Welfare State could guarantee their satisfaction. In public provision, as in individuals' life-styles, choices have to be made, and the public leisure services are no more capable of enabling citizens to transcend the constraints imposed by time, income and domestic responsibilities, than of disentangling their own priorities from the political structures that supply their finance and authority. Given this predicament, however liberal the practitioners' aspirations, is it possible for the leisure services to respond solely to people's interests? Rationalisation could prove less benign than intended. In the past the fragmentation of the leisure industries has helped preserve a measure of consumer sovereignty. Implementing a coherent leisure policy with clear priorities might actually diminish individuals' scope for choice.[17]

Above all else, theories of and policies for leisure need to respect the latter's character. There are grounds for criticising sociologists who draw *exclusively* on well-worn theories of class domination to appraise leisure and its services, and equally 'conservative' non-sociologists who reach for familiar, tried-and-tested formulae in social administration. Leisure has properties that discord with conventional approaches to 'solving social problems'. Attempts to evolve policies for leisure need to begin by pondering the evidence that sociology, and other disciplines, have placed at our disposal. The most important discovery may well be that leisure is not damaging. It is not a problem analogous to crime, disease, poverty and educational underachievement that experts are required to solve, and that the social services need to alleviate. In general, people make a success of leisure's enjoyment. Furthermore, given the processes that account for this enjoyment, providers and other experts must recognise that their contribution will remain incidental. Satisfactions from leisure depend upon people developing and implementing their own rationalities or meanings.

Facility or time-famine?

Demands for action on the leisure front usually start from the assumption that leisure time and its uses are growing problems. Accept this proposition, and it is difficult to resist the case for more arts, sports and community centres, more provision for countryside recreation and education to enable the public to appreciate these facilities. In fact, however, there is not a shred of evidence to support the argument that filling leisure time is a growing problem. Previous chapters have not pointed to this conclusion. One of the great myths of our age is that we are threatened by a wilderness of spare time.

Work-free lifetime has grown, but more slowly than income and spending on leisure goods and services. Leisure time, therefore, has become *relatively* scarce rather than plentiful. Lifetime is a scarce resource. It is the classic scarce resource in that its supply, in the short-term, is absolutely fixed. No one can purchase more than 24 hours per day, or 7 days per week. The historical trends are not towards an age of gracious or boring idleness. Rather than 'filling time', our growing problem is 'finding the time'. It is the 'harried leisure class' that is expanding.[18] Among certain sections of the population, particularly the retired and unemployed, complaints of surplus time are common. But larger sections of the public are learning to cope with a 'time-famine' – too few hours per day and days per week to indulge all their interests. Hence the appeal of time-saving and 'time-deepening' leisure activities – fast food rather than 'leisurely' meals, and squash rather than cricket.

A wasteland?

A second great myth is that we find our leisure activities point-less, hollow and frustrating – that our leisure is devoid of mean-ing. Once again, previous chapters have offered no support for this belief. Ralph Glasser has argued that leisure's promise of fulfilment is no more than a romantic fiction.[19] He claims that since leisure is not organised towards any definite ends, its 'en-joyment' becomes a penalty rather than a prize. By compressing more and more activities into our increasingly precious leisure time, Glasser argues, we only generate extreme stress to which there is no known cure.

In fact all the evidence indicates that leisure activity enhances the individual's sense of well-being. In America and Britain the findings are entirely consistent. The number of leisure activities and contacts that individuals report prove positively related to self-rated happiness and satisfaction with life. Satisfaction with leisure correlates positively, and is a major contributor to overall life satisfaction. High involvement in both home-based and out-of-home recreation leads to feelings of accomplishment and creativity, to a sense of being appreciated, and to high levels of social and psychological adjustment.[20] Our methods of measur-ing the quality of life are imperfect.[21] Answers to structured survey questions will not yield *accurate* measures of life satisfac-tion. But the best evidence at our disposal points to the un-equivocal conclusion that leisure *per se* is not a problem. For most people filling leisure time is not difficult, and their leisure activities do not threaten but enhance life's quality.

The leisure enigma

What policy implications follow from most people *not* finding leisure a problem? Apart from there being no call for urgent mass-rescue missions, the direct policy implications are absolute-ly nil. Those seeking to curb public expenditure may be tempted to conclude that provision for leisure is already adequate. But expansionists are equally entitled to infer that the public cannot be given too much of a good thing, and that central and local governments should back a winner, increase provision for leisure and thereby swell the sum total of human happiness.

All attempts to move from evidence about individuals' satisfactions to public recreation policies have to surmount the leisure enigma. Among the public at large, leisure activity is related to well-being; this evidence is unambiguous. Yet attempts to measure the contributions to welfare of public leisure services that are provided free or at subsidised prices to users normally find that the benefits do not justify the outlay. In America Diana Dunn has shown that levels and patterns of spending on public leisure services in different cities are unrelated to indices of social pathology. In contrast, she discovered a definite and positive relationship between 'social health' and mean levels of income.[22] It is difficult to measure the value derived from specific facilities such as playing fields and parks. Economists admit that their instruments are blunt. All they claim is an advance on intuition. One popular technique has been to employ distance travelled to estimate the price members of the public would be prepared to pay to use a facility. Add the number of users to the equation, and a cash estimate of total public benefit can be derived.[23] Such estimates are admittedly 'rule of thumb', like our measures of life's quality.[24] Travelling is a 'cost', but it may also have some positive value. People journey *for* as well as *to* leisure. The car drive can be part of the attraction. In addition, non-users may derive some psychic benefits from the existence and knowledge that others are able to enjoy playing fields, the countryside and high culture. But we cannot simply ignore the conclusions of economists who have endeavoured to measure public benefits: 'Economic considerations alone will rarely justify the provision of public open space against residential, commercial or industrial use of the land.'[25]

If leisure activity in general contributes to well-being, surely the same must be true of the leisure facilities that individuals use. The enigma is perplexing, until we draw the sociological perspectives, developed in previous chapters, into the analysis. Leisure activities are not usually valued for their 'own sake'. Their 'meanings' are crucial. It is largely through socially constructed meanings that leisure contributes to well-being, principally by enabling individuals to express interests, to develop and state their identities. Realising interests and expressing identities *directly* raise life satisfaction. Leisure activities contribute indirectly, through the meanings they possess for actors and their audiences.[26] As argued in earlier chapters, there need be no 1 : 1 relationship between people's interests and activities, and an implication is that while particular sports and forms of countryside recreation may make important contributions to many individuals' life-styles, if the specific facilities they current-ly use were not available, the relevant interests would simply find alternative means of expression. Furthermore, satisfactions from leisure derive largely from individuals identifying and ex-pressing their *own* interests, and building their *own* connections with their environments.[27] For the recreation professions, the planners and providers, the implication is that their role in lei-sure is fundamentally incidental. They can cater for as many activities as possible, disseminate knowledge and thereby help to break down social barriers to participation. But at the end of the day it is ordinary people with leisure who must define their in-terests and identities, and establish connections with their physical and social environments. In the final analysis, indi-viduals' ability to use leisure to enhance their quality of life de-pends less on the providers of recreation facilities than the other resources at their disposal, mainly time and money, but also self-confidence, the distribution of which is not in the hands of the recreation professions.

A leisure perspective in social policy

Rather than underwriting calls for strengthening specialist lei-sure services, a sociological perspective makes a more persuasive case for taking leisure into account across a wider range of so-cial, economic and manpower policies. It explains why greater leisure provision may not always be the most enlightened re-sponse to the growing challenge of leisure. Trade unions are now aware that the working class is under-represented in most forms of out-of-home recreation, and have called for low-cost-to-the-user facilities to be targeted towards disadvantaged areas, with instructors to overcome inhibitions, and community involve-ment in management and planning to encourage participation by local residents.[28] Trade union spokesmen's hearts are un-doubtedly on their members' side, but our evidence indicates that the main beneficiaries of these proposals would not be the working class. The middle classes prove more likely to involve themselves in management and planning, to use instructors and low-cost facilities, even when this means journeying into inner-city districts such as Manchester's Moss Side. Geographical proximity is not a powerful predictor of recreational behaviour. Leisure activity is most limited among individuals handicapped by age, gender and low income, and the best way of extending their leisure opportunities would be through addressing these disadvantages. Women need liberating from gender constraints, poor people need money and the unemployed need jobs, not specially designed leisure services. Leisure is not overriding, but confirming our need to tackle long-standing problems rooted in the ageing process, inequalities in industry and income distribution and the domestic division of labour. If these issues can be resolved, leisure will largely take care of itself.

All systematic analyses demonstrate that leisure is a complex phenomenon. In certain senses it is just a part, in others a pervasive quality of life. Leisure is composed from a variety of elements. No serious analysts endorse the simple equation that life minus work equals leisure. Individuals need other resources, particularly income, to 'mix' with free time before they can express their interests and identities. An implication is that if, as seems likely, work-free lifetime will continue to increase, and if we want a result to be a growth of leisure which enhances the quality of life, we need to ensure that the relevant free time is distributed appropriately. We have been warned that, 'Microprocessors are far more likely to divide the nation into those in full-time work and the unemployed than to produce a general reduction in working hours, because that is how the labour market functions'.[29] This is how the labour market ordinarily operates since, for employers, it is usually cheaper and more convenient to adjust to changes in technology and demand by managing overtime than by renegotiating 'normal' working hours. We could face a future in which most of us, the better educated, qualified and trained, will continue to be fully employed throughout our adult lives, while a growing minority, the untrained and unqualified, are sentenced to lifetimes of subemployment in low-paid occupations, on the margins of the economy and society. The recreation professions will be unable to repair the damage. The growth of satisfying leisure will depend upon how trade unions use their bargaining power, and whether governments use their influence to spread the benefits of work and free time equitably.

Leisure and recreation are not synonymous. Spare time and income are not always devoted to fun and games. Previous chapters have emphasised that time released from paid employment is often devoted to other types of 'work' – mainly in the home, but also in education, voluntary associations and politics. For individuals who are excluded from the formal labour force, these alternative types of work can assume the functions ordinarily performed by paid employment. They can structure time, offer individuals 'status' as a reward for their 'work' and thereby provide satisfying identities. The unemployed may gain more from opportunities to undertake alternative forms of work than from privileged access to leisure centres. Leisure opportunities need not mean recreation facilities, and governments conversant with leisure's properties will be alert to the case for responding to any contraction of the labour force by supporting other types of work.

There is a demand for recreation, and its satisfaction contributes to life's quality. Research endorses these propositions. But exactly how much to spend on public recreation, and the balance to strike between the arts, sport and countryside recreation are questions that cannot be answered from the current evidence. The knowledge at our disposal does not make us omniscient. When researchers call for greater provision they speak as citizens, which is their right, not as representatives of their disciplines. Sociology's findings and arguments supply no grounds for slashing the public leisure services. The situation is simply that, for the present, decisions on levels and forms of provision must continue to depend heavily on the 'common sense' of democratically elected representatives. If and when we learn more about the meanings, motivations and gratifications that inspire different patterns of leisure activity, researchers' policy recommendations may increase in precision. In the meantime declaring the traditional democratic channels redundant would be premature. Sociology's present contribution is to open issues for further investigation, and for debate, not only among the recreation professions, but across a wider range of social and economic policies.

REFERENCES AND FURTHER READING

Chapter 1 Leisure and sociology

1. F. M. Andrews and S. B. Withey, *Social Indicators of Well-being*, Plenum Press, New York, 1976.
2. Department of the Environment, *Leisure and the Quality of Life*, Vols 1 and 2, HMSO, 1977.
3. Sports Council, Research Working Papers, 7, *Sport and Recreation in the Inner City*, 1978.
4. M. A. Smith (ed.), *Directory of Leisure Scholars and Research*, Centre for Leisure Studies and Research, University of Salford, 1980.
5. G. Godbey, *Recreation, Park and Leisure Services*, Saunders, Philadelphia, 1978.
6. D. R. Dunn, 'Recreation in the urbanising world: no models to mimic', *Society and Leisure*, 1976.
7. British Travel Association/University of Keele, *Pilot National Recreation Survey*, 1967; K. Sillitoe, *Planning for Leisure*, HMSO, 1969; North West Sports Council, *Leisure in the North West*, 1972; Countryside Commission, *National Survey of Countryside Recreation*, 1980.
8. A. J. Veal, *Leisure and Recreation in England and Wales, 1973*, Countryside Commission, 1976; A. J. Veal, *Sport and Recreation in England and Wales: An analysis of adult participation patterns in 1977*, Centre for Urban and Regional Studies, University of Birmingham, 1979.
9. Social Science Research Council/Sports Council, *Report of the Joint Working Party on Recreation Research*, 1978.

Chapter 2 Leisure and industrialism

1. J. Huizinga, *Homo Ludens*, Routledge, 1949.
2. P. C. McIntosh, *Sport in Society*, Watts, 1963.
3. D. Brailsford, *Sport and Society*, Routledge, 1969.
4. S. de Grazia, *Of Time, Work and Leisure*, Twentieth Century Fund, New York, 1962.
5. As argued by N. J. Cheek, Jnr and W. R. Burch, Jnr, *The Social Organisation of Leisure in Human Society*, Harper and Row, New York, 1976.
6. R. W. Malcolmson, *Popular Recreations in English Society 1700–1850*, Cambridge University Press, 1973, p. 1.

7. *Ibid.*, p. 5.
8. *Ibid.*, p. 89.
9. Quoted in J. Myerscough, 'The recent history and use of leisure time', in I. Appleton (ed.), *Leisure Research and Policy*, Scottish Academic Press, 1974.
10. *Ibid.*
11. See J. Walvin, *Leisure and Society 1830–1950*, Longman, 1978.
12. A. A. Harris, *Sport in Greece and Rome*, Thames and Hudson, 1972.
13. J. Neulinger, 'A report of and comments on the symposium reasons for leisure: research of factors which influence leisure behaviour', *Leisure Newsletter*, 1979, 7, 6.
14. J. F. Murphy, *Concepts of Leisure*, Prentice-Hall, New Jersey, 1974.

Chapter 3 The growth of leisure

1. *New Survey on London Life and Labour*, Vol. 9, 'Life and Labour', King, 1935.
2. M. A. Bienefeld, *Working Hours in British Industry*, Weidenfeld and Nicolson, 1972.
3. J. M. Kreps, *Lifetime Allocation of Work and Income*, Duke University Press, North Carolina, 1971; M. Kaplan, *Leisure: Theory and Policy*, Wiley, New York, 1975.
4. J. I. Gershuny and G. S. Thomas, *Changing Patterns of Time Use: UK activity patterns in 1961 and 1975*, Science Policy Research Unit, University of Sussex, 1979.
5. A. Hawkins and J. Lowerson, *Trends in Leisure 1919–1939*, Social Science Research Council/Sports Council, 1979.
6. W. H. Martin and S. Mason, *Broad Patterns of Leisure Expenditure*, Leisure Consultants, 1979.
7. D. Barker, 'Young People and their homes', *Sociological Review*, 20, 1972, 569.
8. J. Walvin, *Leisure and Society 1830–1950*, Longman, 1978; P. Bailey, *Leisure and Class in Victorian England*, Routledge, 1978.
9. See H. E. Meller, *Leisure and the Changing City 1870–1914*, Routledge, 1976.
10. A. Delgado, *Victorian Entertainment*, David and Charles, 1971.
11. D. Dallas, *The Travelling People*, Macmillan, 1971.
12. Walvin, *Leisure and Society*.
13. A. Delgado, *The Annual Outing and other Excursions*, Allen and Unwin, 1977.
14. S. Howell, *The Seaside*, Studio Vista, 1974.
15. J. Walvin, *Beside the Seaside*, Allen Lane, 1978.
16. L. Turner and J. Ash, *The Golden Hordes*, Constable, 1975.
17. A. J. Burkart and S. Medlik, *Tourism*, Heinemann, 1974.
18. Turner and Ash, *op. cit*; D. E. Davis, 'Development of the tourist industry in third world countries', *Society and Leisure*, 1, 1978, 301.
19. E. Dunning, 'The development of modern football', in E. Dunning (ed.), *The Sociology of Sport*, Frank Cass, 1971; *The Development of a Major Spectator Sport*, Social Science Research Council/Sports Council, 1979; N. Elias and E. Dunning, 'Folk football in medieval England and early modern Britain', in Dunning (ed.), *op. cit.*

20. See J. Walvin, *The People's Game*, Allen Lane, 1975.
21. *Ibid.*
22. E. Dunning and K. Sheard, *Barbarians, Gentlemen and Players*, Martin Robertson, 1979.
23. Bailey, *op. cit.*
24. Walvin, *Leisure and Society*.
25. F. Coalter, 'Leisure and ideology', *Leisure Studies Association Quarterly*, 1, 1980 6; J. Henderson, 'Leisure and social discipline', *ibid.*, 9.
26. A. W. Bacon, 'The embarrassed self', *Society and Leisure*, 4, 1972, 23.
27. A. Clayre, *Work and Play*, Weidenfeld and Nicolson, 1975.
28. Meller, *op. cit.*

Chapter 4 Contemporary Britain at play

1. W. H. Martin and S Mason, *Broad Patterns of Leisure Expenditure*, Leisure Consultants, 1979.
2. Countryside Commission, *Study of Informal Recreation in South East England*, 1977.
3. A. J. Veal, *Sport and Recreation in England and Wales: An analysis of adult participation patterns in 1977*, Centre for Urban and Regional Studies, University of Birmingham, 1979.
4. *Ibid.*
5. *Ibid.*
6. M. Young and P. Willmott, *The Symmetrical Family*, Routledge, 1973.
7. Martin and Mason, *op. cit.*
8. M. Bradley and D. Fenwick, *Popular Attitudes to Liquor Licensing Laws in Great Britain*, HMSO, 1974.
9. *Ibid.*
10. Home Office, *Gambling Statistics: Great Britain 1968–78*, 1980.
11. *Report of the Royal Commission on Gambling*, HMSO, 1978.
12. Home Office, *op. cit.*
13. J. Halliday and P. Fuller (eds), *The Psychology of Gambling*, Penguin, 1977.
14. D. Oldman, 'Compulsive gamblers', *Sociological Review*, 26, 1978, 349; D. B. Cornish, *Gambling: A review of the literature*, HMSO, 1978.
15. O. Newman, *Gambling: Hazard and reward*, Athlone Press, 1972.
16. A. J. Veal, *Leisure and Recreation in England and Wales, 1973*, Countryside Commission, 1976.
17. Veal, *Sport and Recreation in England and Wales*.
18. *Ibid.*
19. E. C. Bammel, 'Wilderness and urban society', in M. A. Smith (ed.), *Leisure and Urban Society*, Leisure Studies Association, 1977.
20. S. Hall *et al.*, *Fads and Fashions*, Social Science Research Council/Sports Council, 1979.
21. N. Petrysak, 'The appeal of violence in spectator sport – a bio-sociological perspective', in M. A. Smith (ed.), *op. cit.*
22. J. Walvin, *The People's Game*, Allen Lane, 1975.
23. I. R. Taylor, 'Soccer consciousness and soccer hooliganism', in S. Cohen (ed.), *Images of Deviance*, Penguin, 1971.
24. P. Marsh *et al.*, *Aggro: The illusion of violence*, Dent, 1978; *The Rules of Disorder*, Routledge, 1978.

25. See J. Clarke, *Football hooliganism and the skinheads*, Occasional Paper, Centre for Contemporary Cultural Studies, University of Birmingham, 1977; R. Ingham, *Football Hood: The Wider Context*, Interaction Imprint, 1978; D. Robins and P. Cohen, *Knuckle Sandwich*, Penguin, 1978.
26. North West Sports Council, *Leisure in the North West*, 1972.
27. Countryside Commission, *op. cit.*
28. *Ibid.*
29. J. I. Gershuny and G. S. Thomas, *Changing Patterns of Time Use: UK activity patterns in 1961 and 1975*, Science Policy Research Unit, University of Sussex, 1979.
30. W. Bacon, *Time for Leisure*, Countryside Commission, 1979.
31. H. G. Brown, 'Some effects of shift work on social and domestic life', *Yorkshire Bulletin of Economic and Social Research*, Occasional Paper 2, 1959; P. E. Mott *et al.*, *Shift Work; The Social, Psychological and Physical Consequences*, University of Michigan Press, 1965,
32. Martin and Mason, *op. cit.*
33. Countryside Commission, *op. cit.*; J. White and M. Dunn, *Recreational Use of the Countryside: A case study in the West Midlands*, Research Memorandum 33, Centre for Urban and Regional Studies, University of Birmingham, 1974.
34. South West Economic Planning Council, *Economic Survey of the Tourist Industry in the South-West*, HMSO, 1976.
35. Countryside Commission, *op. cit.*
36. H. Swedner, 'The Swedish experience: life and leisure in an affluent mixed economy', in G. E. Cherry and A. S. Travis (eds), *Leisure in the 1980s: Alternative futures*, Leisure Studies Association, 1980.
37. A. Delgado, *Victorian Entertainment*, David and Charles, 1971.
38. Bradley and Fenwick, *op. cit.*
39. Gershuny and Thomas, *op. cit.*
40. Bacon, *op. cit.*; and *Holidays and Countryside Recreation*, Countryside Commission, 1979.
41. D. Rust, *Dance and Society*, Routledge, 1969.

Chapter 5 Work and leisure

1. N. Dennis *et al.*, *Coal is our Life*, Tavistock, 1956.
2. G. Friedmann, *The Anatomy of Work*, Heinemann, 1961.
3. W. H. Whyte, *The Organisation Man*, Cape, 1956.
4. C. Wright Mills, *White Collar*, Galaxy, New York, 1956.
5. A. Piepe *et al.*, *Television and the Working Class*, Saxon House, 1975.
6. Tourism and Recreation Research Unit, *A Research Study into Recreation Activity Substitution in Scotland*, University of Edinburgh, 1977.
7. L. Reisman, 'Class, leisure and social participation', *American Sociological Review*, **19**, 1954, 76; H. H. Hyman and C. R. Wright, 'Trends in voluntary association memberships of American adults', *ibid.*, **36**, 1971, 191.
8. Countryside Commission, *National Survey of Countryside Recreation*, 1980.
9. W. Bacon, *Time for Leisure*, Countryside Commission, 1979.
10. *Ibid.*
11. A. J. Veal, *Sport and Recreation in England and Wales: An analysis of adult participation patterns in 1977*, Centre for Urban and Regional Studies, University of Birmingham, 1979.

12. M. Collins and B. Rees, 'Sport in an urban context' in S. Parker *et al.* (eds), *Sport and Leisure in Contemporary Society*, Polytechnic of Central London, 1975.
13. Countryside Commission, *Study of Informal Recreation in South East England*, 1977.
14. A. C. Clarke, 'The use of leisure and its relation to levels of occupational prestige', *American Sociological Review*, 21, 1956, 301.
15. J. E. Gerstl, 'Leisure, taste and occupational miheu', in E. O. Smigel (ed.), *Work and Leisure*, College and University Press, New Haven, 1963.
16. R. Taylor, 'Marilyn's friends and Rita's customers', *Sociological Review*, 26, 1978, 573.
17. J. Child and B. Macmillan, 'Managers and their leisure', in M. A. Smith *et al.* (eds), *Leisure and Society in Britain*, Allen Lane, 1973.
18. S. Parker, *The Future of Work and Leisure*, MacGibbon and Kee, 1971.
19. J. E. Champoux, 'Perceptions of work and non-work', *Sociology of Work and Occupations*, 5, 1978, 402.
20. G. Salaman, *Community and Occupation*, Cambridge University Press, 1974.
21. J. H. Goldthorpe *et al.*, *The Affluent Worker, 1, Industrial Attitudes and Behaviour*, Cambridge University Press, 1968.
22. G. A. Allan, *A Sociology of Friendship and Kinship*, Allen and Unwin, 1979.
23. H. L. Wilenski, 'Orderly careers and social participation', *American Sociological Review*, 26, 1961, 521.
24. R. Lansbury, 'Careers, work and leisure among the new professionals', *Sociological Review*, 22, 1974, 385.
25. P. Golding, *The Mass Media*, Longman, 1974, p. 15.
26. See L. F. Pearson, *Working Life and Leisure*, Sunderland Polytechnic, 1977.
27. R. Dubin, 'The industrial worker's world: a study of the central life interests of industrial workers', *Social Problems*, 3, 1956, 131.
28. J. R. Kelly, 'Situational and social factors in leisure decisions', *Pacific Sociological Review*, 21, 1978, 317.
29. B. Bacon, 'Leisure and the craftworkers', in M. A. Smith (ed.) *op.cit.*
30. J. Dumazedier, *Sociology of Leisure*, Elsevier, Amsterdam, 1974.
31. J. R. Kelly, *op. cit.*
32. T. Burns, 'Leisure in industrial society', in Smith *et al.* (eds), *op. cit.*
33. N. Anderson, *Work and Leisure*, Routledge, 1967.
34. F. Best (ed.) *The Future of Work*, Prentice-Hall, New Jersey, 1976.
35. J. Dumazedier, *op. cit.*
36. R. K. Brown *et al.*, 'Leisure in work', in Smith *et al.* (eds), *op. cit.*
37. D. Guest and R. Williams, 'How home affects work', *New Society*, 18.1.73.
38. E. Clark, 'Life in the middle', *New Society*, 11.1.73.
39. F. Best, 'The time of our lives', *Society and Leisure*, 1, 1978, 95.
40. J. de Chalendar, *Lifelong Allocation of Time*, Organisation for Economic Co-operation and Development, Paris, 1976.

Chapter 6 Leisure and the family

1.   B. J. Rees and M. F. Collins, 'The family and sport: a review', in Z. Strelitz (ed.), *Leisure and Family Diversity*, Leisure Studies Association, 1979.
2.   E. H. Scheuch, 'Family cohesion in leisure time', *Sociological Review*, 8, 1960, 37.

3. M. Elson, 'The weekend car', *New Society*, 11.4.74.
4. B. J. Rees and M. F. Collins, *op. cit.*
5. N. Cheek *et al.*, *Leisure and Recreation Places*, Ann Arbor Science, 1976.
6. J. Streather, 'One-parent families and leisure', in Strelitz (ed.), *op. cit.*
7. K. E. Rosengren and S. Windahl, 'Mass media consumption as a functional alternative', in D. McQuail (ed.), *The Sociology of Mass Communications*, Penguin, 1972.
8. K. Sillitoe, *Planning for Leisure*, HMSO, 1969.
9. P. Willmott, *Adolescent Boys of East London*, Routledge, 1966.
10. M. Abrams, *The Teenage Consumer*, London Press Exchange, 1961.
11. IPC Magazines, *Teenagers and Young Housewives: A study of their markets, 1972, 1973.*
12. W. A. Belson, *The Impact of Television*, Crosby Lockwood, 1967.
13. R. and R. N. Rapoport, *Leisure and the Family Life-cycle*, Routledge, 1975.
14. J. R. Kelly, 'Leisure adaptation to family variety', in Strelitz (ed.), *op. cit.*
15. Tourism and Recreation Research Unit, *Report on Aspects of the Results from the NSCR*, Countryside Commission, 1978.
16. R. J. Estes and H. Wilenski, 'Life-cycle squeeze and the morale curve', *Institute of Industrial Relations Reprint*, No. 422, University of California, 1978.
17. D. Hobson, 'Working class women, the family and leisure', in Strelitz (ed.), *op. cit.*
18. J. Long, 'Retirement, leisure and the family', in Strelitz (ed.), *op. cit*; J. Long and E. Wimbush, *Leisure and the Over-50s*, Social Science Research Council/Sports Council, 1979.
19. S. Parker, 'Retirement – leisure or not?' *Society and Leisure*, **2**, 1979 329.
20. M. Kaplan, *Leisure: Lifestyle and lifespan*, Saunders, Philadelphia, 1979.
21. Parker, *op. cit.*
22. L. Stanley, 'Sex, gender and the sociology of leisure', in M. A. Smith (ed.), *Leisure and Urban Society*, Leisure Studies Association, 1977.
23. Hobson, *op. cit.*
24. See M. Talbot, *Women and Leisure*, Social Science Research Council/Sports Council, 1979.
25. A. Tomlinson, 'Leisure, the family and the woman's role', in Strelitz (ed.), *op. cit.*
26. Belson, *op. cit.*
27. I. Cullen, 'A day in the life of . . .' *New Society*, 11.4.74.
28. J. I. Gershuny and G. S. Thomas, *Changing Patterns of Time Use: UK activity patterns in 1961 and 1975*, Science Policy Research Unit, University of Sussex, 1979.
29. P. Hunt, 'Cash transactions and household tasks', *Sociological Review*, 1978, **26**, 555.
30. See N. C. A. Parry and D. Johnson, *Leisure and Social Structure*, Hatfield Polytechnic, 1974.
31. E. Derrick *et al.*, *School-children and Leisure: Interim report*, Working Paper 19, Centre for Urban and Regional Studies, University of Birmingham, 1973; S. Sharpe, *Just Like a Girl*, Penguin, 1977.
32. E. A. Douvan and J. Adelson, *The Adolescent Experience*, Wiley, New York, 1966.
33. C. Octon, 'Leisure in mid-life', in Strelitz (ed.), *op. cit.*
34. A. Booth, 'Sex and social participation', *American Sociological Review*, **37**, 1972, 183.

35. Talbot, *op. cit.*
36. C. Bell and P. Healey, 'The family and leisure', in M. A. Smith *et al.* (eds), *Leisure and Society in Britain*, Allen Lane, 1973.
37. R. O. Blood and D. M. Wolfe, *Husbands and Wives*, Free Press, Glencoe, 1965.
38. J. R. Kelly, 'Leisure adaptation to family variety'.
39. *Ibid.*
40. Parry and Johnson, *op. cit.*
41. J. R. Kelly, 'Situational and social factors in leisure decisions', *Pacific Sociological Review*, 21, 1978, 131.
42. J. Dumazedier, *Sociology of Leisure*, Elsevier, Amsterdam, 1974.
43. Blood and Wolfe, *op. cit.*
44. M. Kaplan, *Leisure:Theory and Policy*, Wiley, New York, 1975, p. 211.
45. N. Foote, 'Sex as play', *Social Problems*, 1, 1954, 159.
46. M. Wolfenstein, 'The emergence of a fun morality', *Journal of Social Issues*, 7, 1951, 15.
47. J. and E. Newson, *Four Years Old in an Urban Community*, Allen and Unwin, 1968.

Chapter 7 Leisure and the future

1. B. Sherman, 'The technological future and the collapse of work', in G. E. Cherry and A. S. Travis (eds), *Leisure in the 1980s: Alternative futures*, Leisure Studies Association, 1980.
2. T. Stonier, 'Technological change and the future', paper presented to the British Association for the Advancement of Science, Edinburgh, 1979.
3. A. Touraine, *The Post-Industrial Society*, Random House, New York, 1971.
4. D. Bell, *The Coming of Post-Industrial Society*, Basic Books, New York, 1974.
5. P. Halmos, *The Personal Service Society*, Constable, 1970.
6. W. Bennis and P. Slater, *The Temporary Society*, Harper and Row, New York, 1968.
7. A. Toffler, *Future Shock*, Random House, New York, 1970.
8. D. E. Guest, *Work and Careers in the Years up to 2000*, Institute of Careers Officers, 1977.
9. F. Best, 'The time of our lives', *Society and Leisure*, 1, 1978, 95.
10. P. Goldring, *Multipurpose Man*, Dent, 1973.
11. F. Best (ed.), *The Future of Work*, Prentice-Hall, New Jersey, 1976.
12. G. Palm, *The Flight from Work*, Cambridge University Press, 1977.
13. B. Abrahamsson, *Bureaucracy or Participation*, Sage, 1973, p. 228.
14. Best, 'The time of our lives'.
15. Best (ed.), *The Future of Work*.
16. R. E. Farson, 'A Bill of Rights for 1984', *New Society*, 12.6.69.
17. *Ibid.*
18. Central Policy Review Staff, *Social and Employment Implications of Microelectronics*, 1978.
19. S. Parker, *The Future of Work and Leisure*, MacGibbon and Kee, 1971.
20. See J. Tyler, 'The ecological alternative: a socio-political scenario', in Cherry and Travis (eds), *op. cit.*.
21. See K. Kumar, *Prophecy and Progress*, Penguin, 1978.
22. D. H. Meadows *et al.*, *The Limits to Growth*, Club of Rome, New York, 1972.

23. R. E. Miles, *Awakening from the American Dream*, Marion Boyars/Open Forum, 1977.
24. R. L. Heilbronner, *Business Civilisation in Decline*, Marion Boyars, 1976.
25. C. Freeman and M. Jahoda (eds), *World Futures*, Martin Robertson, 1978, p. 6.
26. A. Sauvy, *Zero Growth*, Blackwell, 1975.
27. F. Hirsch, *The Social Limits to Growth*, Routledge, 1977.
28. *Ibid.*, p. 5.
29. E. A. Tiryakian, 'The time perspectives of modernity', *Society and Leisure*, 1, 1978, 125.
30. I. Illich, *The Right to Useful Unemployment*, Marion Boyars, 1978.
31. O. Newman, 'Leisure and lifestyle', *Ontario Psychologist*, 8, 1976, 28.
32. F. Inglis, *The Name of the Game*, Heinemann, 1977.
33. D. MacCannell, *The Tourist*, Macmillan, 1976.
34. J. Dumazedier, *Sociology of Leisure*, Elsevier, Amsterdam, 1974.
35. M. Kaplan, *Leisure in America*, Wiley, New York, 1960.
36. M. Kaplan, *Leisure: Theory and policy*, Wiley, New York, 1975.
37. J. Nisbet, Foreword to L. B. Hendry, *School, Sport and Leisure*, Lepus Books, 1978.
38. J. T. Haworth (ed.), *Community Involvement and Leisure*, Lepus Books, 1979.
39. S. Braden, *Artists and People*, Routledge, 1978; R. R. Clark, *The Arts Council*, Centre for Leisure Studies and Research, University of Salford, 1980.
40. G. Pronovost, 'La Recherche en loisir et le développement culturel', *Society and Leisure*, 1, 1978, 355.
41. C. Perrow, 'Technology, organisations and environment: a cautionary note' *Supplementary Material, DT 353, 15–16*, Open University, 1974.
42. A. Levison, *The Working Class Majority*, Coward, McCann and Geoghegan, 1974.
43. Perrow, *op. cit.*
44. A. Gorz, 'Technical intelligence and the capitalist division of labour', *Telos*, 12, 1972, 27.
45. R. Taylor, 'Marilyn's friends and Rita's customers', *Sociological Review*, 26, 1978, 573.
46. J. M. Kreps, *Lifetime Allocation of Work and Income*, Duke University Press, North Carolina, 1971.
47. H. L. Wilenski, 'The uneven distribution of leisure', in E. O. Smigel (ed.), *Work and Leisure*, College and University Press, New Haven, 1963.
48. J. I. Gershuny and G. S. Thomas, *Changing Patterns of Time Use: UK activity patterns, in 1961 and 1975*, Science Policy Research Unit, University of Sussex, 1979.
49. Bell, *The Coming of Post-Industrial Society*.
50. Central Policy Review Staff, *op. cit.*
51. Association of Professional, Executive, Clerical and Computer Staff, *Office Technology – the Trade Union Response*, 1979.
52. G. Burck, 'There'll be less leisure than you think', *Fortune*, March 1970.
53. G. Katona *et al.*, *Aspirations and Affluence*, McGraw-Hill, New York, 1971; BBC TV, *These Young People*, 30.7.73.
54. M. Young and P. Willmott, *The Symmetrical Family*, Routledge, 1973.
55. *Ibid.*
56. W. A. Faunce, 'Automation and leisure', in Smigel (ed.), *op. cit.*

57. See R. Poor, *4 Days, 40 Hours*, Pan, 1972.
58. J. Gershuny, *After Industrial Society?*, Macmillan, 1978.
59. C. Reich, *The Greening of America*, Penguin, 1972.
60. R. V. Speck, *The New Families*, Tavistock, 1972.
61. F. Musgrove, *Ecstasy and Holiness*, Methuen, 1974.
62. R. Mills, *Young Outsiders*, Routledge, 1973.
63. D. Robins and P. Cohen, *Knuckle Sandwich*, Penguin, 1978.
64. D. Reisman, 'Leisure and work in post-industrial society', in E. Larrabee and R. Meyersohn (eds), *Mass Leisure*, Glencoe Free Press, 1958.
65. Organisation for Economic Co-operation and Development, *New Patterns for Working Time*, Paris, 1973.
66. D. L. Fleuter, *The Workweek Revolution*, Addison-Wesley, Mass, 1975.
67. D. Bell, *The Cultural Contradictions of Capitalism*, Heinemann, 1976.
68. J. F. Murphy, *Concepts of Leisure*, Prentice-Hall, New Jersey, 1974.
69. See P. D. Anthony, *The Ideology of Work*, Tavistock, 1977.

Chapter 8 Policies for leisure

1. *New Survey of London Life and Labour, Vol. 9, Life and Labour*, King, 1935.
2. A. S. Travis, *The State and Leisure Provision*, Social Science Research Council/Sports Council, 1979.
3. N. Kahn, *The Arts Britain Ignores*, Community Relations Commission, 1976; S. Braden, *Artists and People*, Routledge, 1978; R. R. Clark, *The Arts Council*, Centre for Leisure Studies and Research, University of Salford, 1980.
4. *Select Committee of the House of Lords on Sport and Leisure: Second report*, HMSO, 1973.
5. W. H. Martin and S. Mason, *Broad Patterns of Leisure Expenditure*, Leisure Consultants, 1979.
6. J. A. Blackie *et al.*, *Leisure Planning Process*, Tourism and Recreation Research Unit, University of Edinburgh, 1979.
7. C. S. Van Doren and L. Hodges, *America's Park and Recreation Heritage*, US Department of the Interior, 1975; G. Godbey and S. Parker, *Leisure Studies and Services: An overview*, Saunders, Philadelphia, 1976.
8. Blackie *et al.*, *op. cit.*
9. C. Smith, 'The emergence of leisure as a policy issue for central government and the administrative response', in S. Parker and J. Haworth (eds), *Leisure and Public Policy*, Leisure Studies Association, 1975.
10. Travis, *op. cit.*
11. S. Mennell, *Cultural Policy in Towns*, Council of Europe, Strasbourg, 1976.
12. K. Roberts, *Sociology and Leisure Research*, Centre for Leisure Studies and Research, University of Salford, 1980.
13. See K. Roberts, *Contemporary Society and the Growth of Leisure*, Longman, 1978.
14. F. Coalter, 'Leisure and ideology', *Leisure Studies Association Quarterly*, 1, 1980, 6; J. Henderson, 'Leisure and social discipline', *ibid.*, p. 9.
15. J. Hargreaves, 'The political economy of mass sport', in S. Parker *et al.* (eds), *Sport and Leisure in Contemporary Society*, Polytechnic of Central London, 1975; R. S. Gruneau, 'Sport, social differentiation and social ine-

quality', in D. W. Ball and J. W. Loy (eds), *Sport and Social Order*, Addison-Wesley, Mass, 1975.

16. D. C. Anderson and W. W. Sharrock, 'Biasing the news', *Sociology*, **13**, 1979, 367.

17. See G. Godbey, 'The professionalisation of recreation and parks in the public sector', *Society and Leisure*, **1**, 1978, 269.

18. S. Linder, *The Harried Leisure Class*, Columbia University Press, 1970.

19. R. Glasser, *Leisure: Penalty or prize?*, Macmillan, 1970.

20. D. L. Phillips, 'Social participation and happiness', *American Journal of Sociology*, **72**, 1967, 479; F. M. Andrews and S. B. Withey, *Social Indicators of Well-being*, Plenum Press, 1976; R. J. Havighurst and K. Feigenbaum, 'Leisure and lifestyle', *American Journal of Sociology*, **64**, 1959, 396; Department of the Environment, *Leisure and the Quality of Life*, vols 1 and 2, HMSO, 1977; M. Dower *et al.*, *Leisure Provision and People's Needs*, DART/IFER, Devon, 1980.

21. M. Abrams, 'Quality of life studies', in M. A. Smith (ed.), *Leisure in Urban Society*, Leisure Studies Association, 1977.

22. D. R. Dunn, 'Recreation in the urbanising world: no models to mimic', *Society and Leisure*, 1976.

23. M. Clawson and J. L. Knetsch, *The Economics of Outdoor Recreation*, Johns Hopkins Press, New York, 1966.

24. For a critique see R. W. Vickerman, 'Economics and leisure studies', in M. A. Talbot and R. W. Vickerman (eds), *Social and Economic Costs and Benefits of Leisure*, Leisure Studies Association, 1978.

25. I. M. Seeley, *Outdoor Recreation and the Urban Environment*, Macmillan, 1973, p. 73; see also G. A. C. Searle (ed.), *Recreational Economics and Analysis*, Longman, 1975.

26. See Dower *et al.*, *op. cit.*

27. *Ibid.*

28. Trade Union Congress, *Statement on Participation in Sport and Recreation*, 1980.

29. J. Tyler, 'The ecological alternative: a socio-political scenario', in G. E. Cherry and A. S. Travis (eds), *Leisure in the 1980s: Alternative futures*, Leisure Studies Association, 1980.

Further reading

D. W. Ball and J. W. Loy (eds), *Sport and Social Order*, Addison-Wesley, Mass, 1975.

F. Best (ed.), *The Future of Work*, Prentice-Hall, New Jersey, 1976.

N. J. Cheek, Jnr and W. R. Burch, Jnr, *The Social Organisation of Leisure in Human Society*, Harper and Row, New York, 1976.

J. Dumazedier, *Sociology of Leisure*, Elsevier, Amsterdam, 1974.

R. Glasser, *Leisure: Penalty or prize?*, Macmillan, 1970.

J. T. Haworth and M. A. Smith (eds), *Work and Leisure*, Lepus Books, 1975.

S. Linder, *The Harried Leisure Class*, Columbia University Press, 1970.

J. F. Murphy, *Concepts of Leisure*, Prentice-Hall, New Jersey, 1974.

S. Parker, *The Future of Work and Leisure*, MacGibbon and Kee, 1971.

R. and R. N. Rapoport, *Leisure and the Family Life-cycle*, Routledge, 1975.

K. Roberts, *Contemporary Society and the Growth of Leisure*, Longman, 1978.

M. A. Smith *et al.* (eds), *Leisure and Society in Britain*, Allen Lane, 1973.

J. Walvin, *Leisure and Society 1830–1950*, Longman, 1978.

M. Young and P. Willmott, *The Symmetrical Family*, Routledge, 1973.

INDEX

CONTEMPORARY SOCIETY AND THE GROWTH OF
LEISURE
Kenneth Roberts
First published 1978

This book challenges the preoccupation with activities and
facilities usually associated with research into recreation.
Contemporary leisure is the product of industrialism and should
not, therefore, be viewed in isolation and the author argues that
it can be fully understood only when seen in a wider social
context.

From this sociological perspective the book systematically
examines the impact of leisure on education, the family, youth
culture and working life. A provocative concluding chapter
considers public policy and provision.

Written in a stimulating and lively style, the book will be of
interest not only to sociologists, but also to leisure practitioners
and others concerned with the quality of contemporary life.

RESOURCES FOR THE WELFARE STATE
John F. Sleeman
First published 1979

This text sets out the economic implications of the welfare state and pays particular attention to the means of raising the resources needed to provide social services and the effects that the use of these resources have on the working of the economy. The author discusses the implications of the rapid expansion of government spending in the early 1970s coupled with Britain's relatively slow economic growth, inflation and balance of payments.

HOUSING AND SOCIAL JUSTICE
Gill Burke
First published 1981

Housing offers so many different dimensions for discussion. This book provides a basic introduction to housing and housing policy in Britain and examines how the various sectors have developed, the problems these developments have caused and the part policy has played in their change. It looks at the causes and effects of bad housing and housing shortage with particular reference to homelessness, squatting and rural and urban deprivation. The final section evaluates recent housing policy with reference to social justice. The author challenges the role of social policy in achieving a fair distribution of welfare resources. A large section of the book contains documentary material to provide both evidence and stimulation.

The text is aimed at students taking social policy or social work courses at first year undergraduate or diploma level. It can also be used as an introduction for students in other disciplines and on professional courses.

THE ELDERLY IN MODERN SOCIETY
Anthea Tinker
First published 1981

Economic constraints combined with the projected large increase in the numbers of frail elderly pose difficult problems for families and policy makers in the next two or three decades. By taking into account a wide range of literature from medicine, architecture, sociology, psychology and social policy media, this book presents an account of the present situation and analyses some of the problems and options for the future. The author suggests that families and voluntary bodies will have to play an even greater part than they already do in family care and that realistic supportive services are necessary. In contrast it is also noted that many elderly people require little in the way of services and their contribution to society is greatly underestimated. The book also includes a summary of recent major surveys with views of the effect of recent changes in the organisation of the social services on the elderly.

This text is aimed at students studying degree and diploma courses in social policy. It also presents a reappraisal of society's responsibilities towards the elderly, and will stimulate great interest among social workers, trainee social workers, and the general public.

THE LIMITATIONS OF SOCIAL RESEARCH
second edition
Marten Shipman
First published 1973, this edition 1981

There is an ever increasing output of social science research
producing evidence on which to base action, but not all research
is reliable. The purpose of this book is to provide a consumer's
guide for the majority who read and use the results of research,
rather than the minority who are producing it. It shows how to
assess the credibility of research and probes into the credentials
of the researchers and the bias of their political views. As the
most influential research is often the least reliable, it is of
particular importance that this book is concerned with the
factors affecting the production of evidence and developing
ways of ensuring that the public have the knowledge to make
informed judgements themselves. Each chapter is preceded by
an educational controversy and shows how evidence can support
conflicting situations.

POLITICS TODAY
Edited by Bernard Crick and Patrick Seyd

This paperback series introduces the general reader and the student to the main issues of modern British politics in such a way that the reader can gain a reliable account of how an issue arose, of its institutional context and then discuss what should be done.

THE SELF CONCEPT
Theory, Measurement, Development and Behaviour
R. B. Burns
First published 1979

The self concept – the individual and evaluative image we each have of ourselves – is becoming an increasingly important area of study in psychology and education. This book brings together much hitherto scattered information to provide a comprehensive introduction to the subject. The first section provides historical background, the second deals with how to measure the self concept, in the third section the author details the development of the self concept in the individual and the final section explores behavioural effects. This book will be of immense value to students of education and psychology as well as to a wide range of professionals in the 'helping services', both trainee and practising.

PERSONALITY AND HEREDITY
an introduction to psychogenetics
Brian W. P. Wells
First published 1980

Some of the most acrimonious and crucial scientific controversies of recent years have been concerned with the genetic transmission of human psychological characteristics, particularly in relation to sex differences, criminal and psychopathic behaviour, racial differences, intelligence and homosexuality.

In *Personality and Heredity* Dr Brian Wells has provided a reliable and clear introduction to the relatively new science of psychogenetics. The wide range of material includes evidence in support of the view that aspects of normal intellectual and temperamental development are not only differentially influenced by genetic mechanisms, but so too are many psychotic, neurotic and personality disorders. The author discusses in detail the question of the social significance of inherited psychological traits and its implications for education and psychiatry, race and sex relations, eugenics and genetic engineering.

This book provides a fascinating guide to inherited characteristics for a wide range of readers concerned, scientifically, practically and intellectually with human behaviour and adjustment.